MW00769512

Engaging, witty and thoughtful. *When the Dogs Bark* will leave you laughing, crying, and thinking about everyday life in new ways.

—Robin Day

If you've ever doubted that an animal can be a soulmate, William Roushey, Jr.'s beautifully realized *When the Dogs Bark* will change your mind and your heart. This book will touch anyone who has ever had an animal enrich their life or is hoping to find one.

—Edward Grinnan,
Editor-in-Chief & Vice President, Guideposts,
and author of *Always By My Side*

Bill's life's journey is told by the influence of man's best friend. He allowed his dogs to help get him through good times and difficult times. Then, taking a spiritual view of his life's journey, it gave him insight of how God gets us through life each and every day. This is the kind of read every animal lover would enjoy reading. Thanks for telling the ongoing story of life with your four-legged friends by your side!

—Reverend Forrest States

*Blessings,
Bill Roushey, Jr.*

For anyone who loves dogs, this book is a must read. Each chapter draws the reader into the story of the author and his dogs as well as the spiritual lessons he learned from them. The scripture references at the end of each chapter remind us of the truths that God provides to guide us through our earthly journey. The author has graciously shared the lessons for Godly living that the Holy Spirit has taught him through the interaction with his beloved pets.

—Dave Leupold, retired public school teacher

Bill Roushey weaves together memories of significant life events, several special canine companions present along the way, and the thought-provoking insights which each provided about faith and the relationship between God and man. Readers who have had the privilege to love, and be loved by, a dog will enjoy the nostalgia and reflections sure to be prompted by each chapter.

—Honna Curtis, author of sacredstrokes.blog

When the Dogs Bark

What My Dogs Taught Me about Relationships

William Roushey, Jr.

ILLUMIFY
MEDIA.COM

When the Dogs Bark

Copyright © 2023 by William Roushey Jr.

Published by
Illumify Media Global
www.IllumifyMedia.com
"Let's bring your book to life!"

Paperback ISBN: 978-1-959099-47-5

Typeset by Jennifer Clark
Cover design by Debbie Lewis

Printed in the United States of America

Contents

Introduction

Sheba was like a life preserver, an unexpected source of help sent as an answer to prayer. The day of my rescue began like any other day. My wife, Patty, and I were traveling to my parents' house using an alternate route than the one we normally took. Being born and raised in western New York, I liked to take different roads from time to time to break up the monotony. On one such road we spotted a sign: Puppies for Sale. We stopped on a whim—all right, maybe I twisted Patty's arm a little. The rational side of my brain lobbied for me to get back in the car and resume my already complicated life. I didn't listen. The moment my eyes fell on the litter of mongrel pups, a desire to possess one crept into my heart.

Patty and I walked away holding hands like a couple of sight-seers ready for the next attraction. The sight of the puppies struck an emotional chord in me, however. My mind would not let me abandon them. After being preoccupied with the thought for what seemed like days afterward, I wondered if Patty felt the same way. The more I talked about having a puppy, the more she realized how badly I wanted one.

With Patty's blessing I pressed twenty-five dollars in the seller's hand. Instantly, a coal-black puppy, more Labrador retriever than anything else, became my responsibility. I named her Sheba, after the mysterious queen of ancient Egypt.

Adding a puppy to our lives changed my outlook on life. Sheba became an instant source of inspiration, much as a newborn does to his or her parents. No matter what obstacle I encountered, I could count on Sheba being there for me on the other side. Each day I looked forward to spending time with her. Every one of those days I was treated to a hero's welcome by a squirming, enthusiastic puppy. She became part of every aspect of our lives.

I love dogs. Maybe it's because they treat me as if I'm the most important person in their world, regardless of how much attention I give them. Dogs I have owned want to be with me every minute and follow me everywhere. Perhaps you've witnessed similar behavior in your pet. Whoever dubbed them "man's best friend" did so for good reason. They are members of our families, playmates for our children, coworkers, rescuers, guides, and guardians. Renowned for their faithfulness and devotion, dogs face even the most mundane tasks with unbridled enthusiasm. If ever there was such a thing as a "perfect" relationship, the love shared between a dog and its owner should be given consideration.

You could make a strong argument that dogs were placed here on the earth by our Creator to teach us something about relationships. If this is true, a dog's devotion could serve as a blueprint, a guide to authentic relationships, including one with Jesus Christ. For most people, it's easy enough to describe the relationship they have with their dog. But how does one characterize their relationship with Jesus?

This is not a book on Christian theology. I am not a pastor nor a university professor. I do love Jesus and love to study God's Word. Through the years, I've discovered dogs have a lot to say about relationships when I've taken the time to watch them and reflect. Their actions speak louder, and carry more weight, than human words.

When the Dogs Bark is a compilation of memorable events, I have experienced with the beloved creatures I've called my friends over the years. The events that follow are true stories. Some of the names have been changed to give certain individuals a measure of anonymity.

I've had the privilege of being humbled by the love and devotion of my dogs. Without a doubt, my relationships with my dogs have made me a better person. It is my hope that you will be inspired by my stories about my pets to watch and learn something about relationships from the one you have with your pet.

ONE

Unexpected Inspiration

I OPENED MY EYES. I was lying down. My surroundings looked unfamiliar, and my thoughts were cloudy as if trapped in a fog. The cramped space around me was drenched in sepia tones, causing me to question if what I saw was real. I tried to account for my muscle stiffness. A warm vapor trailed from my lips and rose like cigarette smoke condensing on a glossy surface directly above my face. I reached up and drew a line through the moisture confirming I wasn't dreaming.

Why was the air so cold? Why was I constrained? My six-foot, 160-pound body flopped like a fish removed from its natural element. I was in a sleeping bag. Yes, I remembered climbing into one last night. When I raised myself up on my elbows, I saw how close the walls and ceiling were, and shook off a wave of claustrophobia.

I decided it was Saturday because the alarm clock hadn't interrupted my sleep. I unwound myself from the sleeping bag and turned to face a warm body lying next to me. The sight of Patty brightened my countenance. After two years of marriage, the fragrance of our love hadn't diminished. The early rays of sunlight leaked through the curtains and cast an angelic glow on her face. In a world of billions of people, how did we manage to find each other? Coincidence? Not to our way of thinking. We believed it was a "God thing."

I chuckled. At that moment it occurred to me just how much Patty resembled a young Linda Ronstadt. She'd certainly give me a hard time if I mentioned it, especially after she found Oliva Newton-John's address in an old book I kept back when I was single. I told her I got it off one of her record albums, to which she responded, "Yeah, right!" But then again, maybe she'd take it as a compliment. We both enjoyed listening to Linda's music. Like Linda, Patty was slim, had a cheeky face, and long dark brown hair. Her bangs tumbled over her forehead to meet her eyes. Off the top of my head, I can think of two notable differences between them, however. Patty's eyes were green, not brown, and I was in love with Patty, not Linda Ronstadt.

Patty's eyelids fluttered, startling me.

"Good morning. What time is it?" she said, stretching out her arms and rapping her fingers on the metal wall above her head. "Ouch!"

"It's almost seven o'clock," I answered.

"It's so cold in here."

"The wind must have blown out the pilot on the heater. I haven't convinced myself to get out of my sleeping bag to deal with it."

"What do you want to do about breakfast?"

"If I remember, it's a choice between eggs and cold cereal."

"*Cold* cereal," she countered, rolling up on her side within inches of my face. Her smile was enthralling. She playfully continued, "I'll take care of breakfast if you get the heater going."

We wrapped ourselves in each other's arms. The embrace lasted for several minutes. Neither of us was in a hurry to let go. I found myself overwhelmed with the thought, *I am who I am because of her love,* and wondered where I would be without her in my life.

Learning to trust Patty completely with my life was difficult at first. I had some bad experiences in junior high and as a freshman in high school. I had been a four-foot-six-inch child waiting for puberty to arrive, walking among boys and girls who had already started to develop. I might as well have had a sign on my back saying, "Bully me." Eventually my body caught up with my age, but I still carried a fear of the unknown into our marriage. It escaped from time to time when my neatly ordered life was bushwhacked by something I wasn't familiar with. Fear made it hard to be vulnerable and completely trust in love. Falling head over heels in love with Patty had kept me from having to reveal this to her so far. I guess I didn't want her to think less of me. But marriage, sharing every moment of one's life with another person, has a way of eventually exposing weaknesses and insecurities. I longed for the day fear would be rendered powerless.

"What are you thinking about, Bill?" Patty asked.

"Just how much you mean to me," I answered, once again dodging the issue. "You're the best thing that's ever happened to me."

We continued our embrace. Tears dripped from Patty's eyes. Drops of heartfelt love ran down her cheeks. We were two exhausted bodies clad in worn-out clothes clinging to one another as if love was our only possession. I held her tight and drank from the well of love her soul offered before we parted with a lingering kiss.

Living out of a camper was certainly more challenging than recreational camping. The literal significance of our marriage vows —"for richer or poorer, for better or worse,"—carried a special significance as my bare feet met the chilly linoleum floor. Fortunately, almost everything in the truck camper was accessible in one stride.

After breakfast I dressed in clothes better suited for the late autumn weather in western New York.

"I'm going to go let Sheba out."

"Can you come back for me in an hour?" Patty asked.

"Dress warm!"

I opened the door of the camper and felt a surge of wind that tried unsuccessfully to rip the doorknob from my hand. I wasted several matches trying to light the pilot and keep it lit, blowing on my hands periodically to keep them warm. When the pilot did light, I wondered how long it would stay lit this time.

Though our living arrangement was arduous, Patty and I felt grateful; you could say we even felt blessed. Her parents, Carlin, and Sandy, let us use their camper and paid the lot rent for us while we stayed in the trailer park.

We chose this arrangement because it was extremely close to the house we were building. We had our sights set on obtaining a Certificate of Occupancy. But time was not on our side. Winter was about to set in, and Patty's parents needed to take their camper back home to winterize it.

My parents, Bill, and Wanda, offered to take us in, but they lived ten miles away from the construction site. Since we didn't want to offend them, we kept the option open. Any construction delays would mean we'd have to take them up on their offer. To keep up the goodwill between us, we occasionally stayed overnight. My childhood home had become a hotel. We checked in, ate a meal or two, and checked out. Graciously, they let us burden them with storing our belongings, which consisted of a few unboxed wedding gifts and what could best be described as college dorm room furnishings. Patty and I felt like vagabonds.

Our path to homeownership began earlier that year on a cold February evening. At the time, we were living in college housing reserved for married students. For much of the previous year, we'd tried to prequalify for a mortgage but without success. The many rejections we received boiled down to my limited work experience and income. My work career had spanned only two years at the time. It started just before Patty and I got engaged, which was one month before I graduated from college. Being head over heels in love, I jumped at the chance to earn slightly more than an entry-level wage at the plastics factory where my father worked. Patty was still a full-time college student. We were young and full of grand ideas and had yet to learn the art of being patient.

I managed to keep our dream of owning a home alive by venturing to the grocery store every Saturday to pick up the weekend edition of the newspaper. I combed through the real estate section ritually, and one day I spotted an advertisement from one of those do-it-yourself home building companies. According to the ad, we could use "sweat equity" to realize our dream of homeownership. Patty and I scheduled a consultation with a gentleman from Miles Homes. We decided it wouldn't cost us anything to hear the man out.

On the agreed-upon day, Patty labored to clean our apartment. In her haste she filled the sugar bowl with salt by mistake and later served it with coffee to our guest. That evening, over salty coffee, the salesman guided us through the major elements of the process. We gazed wide-eyed at each other as he talked. Because her father, Carlin, had experience building homes, the salesman told us we'd be good candidates for the program. We soaked up his pitch like sponges. Naively, we vowed to make it happen without knowing what we were getting into. Carlin cautioned us to move slowly and ask a lot of questions. "If something seems too good to be true," he warned, "it probably is."

Carlin was a generous man of average height in his mid-forties. Patty was Daddy's only girl. It was obvious she got her cheeks from her dad. Carlin loved to eat but kept his weight in check by constantly being involved in someone's home improvement project.

The one thing we lacked in our grand scheme was a piece of land to build on. We enlisted the help of a realtor to help us find an approved building lot. Two months passed and we still couldn't find a build site we could afford. I was getting impatient, unaccustomed to the slow-turning wheels of progress.

It was quite humbling when God stepped in to do a little grandstanding. They say prayer changes things, and I found this to be true in this case because doors began to open. We found a home builder willing to sell us what he called a "straggler," a leftover lot from a larger parcel. Mr. Gilbert not only sold us the lot at a price we could afford, but he also deeded it to us with a small down payment if we agreed to make monthly payments on the property. He also connected us with a friend of his, Curly, who was an equipment contractor. Curly, a bald, gruff man in his late fifties, had the vocabulary of a sinner but the heart of a saint. He handled all our excavation needs at a very reasonable price. One by one, obstacles fell like dominos.

I vividly remember that day in May when we stood on the half-acre plot. Patty and I felt like we'd accomplished something significant. We owned a piece of the planet. There wasn't anything special about the lot. It was a field of weeds, scrub brush, and crabgrass, but it was ours.

After surveying the property, Carlin staked out the four corners of the house. The outline formed by the oak stakes seemed impossibly small compared to the open space around it. Ceremoniously, I followed Patty around the interior of the cordoned-off space holding the blueprints, while she visualized the footprint each room would occupy. She stopped here and there to take in the view as if looking out a window.

In July, Carlin assembled a team of able-bodied family members and friends who came to our property for what the Amish community would call a house-raising. I knew many of them traveled several hours to get here, and I worried if there'd be enough work for everyone. I was so naive. Those I didn't know came as a favor to Carlin, an unwritten form of repayment for the many times he'd helped them.

Sweat dripped off our bodies as we worked under the searing heat of the midsummer sun. We paused for meal breaks prepared by Patty, Sandy, Wanda, and the other women who came with their husbands. When the sun finally touched the horizon, we set up lawn chairs and reminisced about the good old days as the glow of a propane lantern cast its light on everyone's faces. I learned a lot about Patty's family from the stories people told. This was the first time in my life I felt so overwhelmed by the generosity of people. I am inclined to agree with those who say there is no gift more precious than giving your time to someone else.

By Labor Day the exterior of the house was completed. The interior work, however, was just beginning. I resumed my work at the factory, and Patty returned to her studies. Our fall schedules made it feel like she lived in one world, and I lived in another. I had no idea how long it would take us to finish the house. Though I had the help of a few family members and a friend or two, there were also times I felt I was journeying alone. Virtually every evening and weekend were spent working on the house. I became discouraged when I saw the leaves begin to change color. Without heat in the house, we would not be able to live there. We were running out of good weather.

Though exhausted and robbed of my strength, I pressed on. Patty and I battled fiberglass insulation that somehow managed to hang in the air long enough to become lodged in our clothes and skin. Drywall dust coated everything in the house, including our hair and mouths. Our once glamorous dream had become like one of my favorite T-shirts, tattered from being worn too many times.

During these troubled times I prayed that God would provide me with inspiration to see me through to the finish line. I repeated this prayer often, many times out loud. I didn't wring my hands or shake my fist when I talked with the Almighty. If I'd learned anything at all in the past few years, it was that God was always listening. It was His mercy that brought Sheba into our lives. She was the perfect source of inspiration, a creature who would never leave my side and was always with me when Patty wasn't there.

～

I drove down the stretch of gravel we called our driveway. Our unfinished house rose out of the sloping landscape like a castle. My heart swelled with pride when I considered the role I played in shaping the vessel that would hold our hope-filled dreams. The idea began like an ember hidden beneath the ashes of a spent fire, waiting for someone to breathe on it and set it aglow. Patty and I talked about raising our children and growing old together in this place.

The keys in my hand jingled as I bounded up the freshly painted white staircase leading to the side door. A surge of giddiness overwhelmed me as I gripped the doorknob and inserted the key. *This is home*, I thought. A bark erupted when I closed the door behind me.

"Sheba!" I hollered.

Her barking intensified at the sound of my voice. The air inside wasn't as cold as it was outside, but it needed to be a lot warmer for the work we planned to do. I walked down a short hallway that led to two unfinished bedrooms at the rear of the house and lit a portable kerosene heater. The sections of drywall lining the walls, cut, and fitted tightly together, reminded me of a jigsaw puzzle. Today's job entailed covering the seams and nail holes with joint compound. I needed the air to be warm enough for the compound to cure properly.

I retreated down a flight of stairs to Sheba's makeshift kennel in the basement. Her lodging was fashioned out of leftover wooden pallets held in place by two-by-fours. A large cardboard box stuffed with hay made for a cozy den.

Sheba yapped with excitement when I drew near. Her bark wasn't fully developed and occasionally cracked like a teenager going through puberty. Regardless of how it sounded, it served to express the depth of her joy. She bounced on her hind legs trying to close the distance between us when I leaned over the kennel. I scooped her up and pressed her warm body to my chest. She showered my face with kisses. I struggled to hold on to her while she squirmed in my arms unable to contain her excitement. It's a measure of enthusiasm you'd expect from a soul reunited with a loved one after spending considerable time apart.

Sheba raced in tight circles around my legs after I placed her on the floor. I smiled and generated a laugh. Carefully I moved toward the back door of the basement, which granted me access to the backyard. It didn't seem to bother her when she collided with my legs. She was one crazy bundle of energy.

Once in the backyard, Sheba sprinted in wide circles. Serenity blanketed the air as the sun rose above the distant trees. Its rays stretched out like fingers creeping ever closer to us. Sheba put on the brakes when she found a good spot to relieve herself. Once finished, she set her sights on me again. Playfully, she leaped against my legs and dashed away repeating her antics several times. Did she know today was my day off from the factory? Perhaps she did know because I wasn't rushing through my morning routine.

Sheba ventured deeper into the backyard smelling the air and chasing after the scents of creatures long since gone. I squatted when I called to her. She raced to meet me and jumped into my arms almost bowling me over in the process. I inhaled the smell of puppy and stroked her velvet fur. My mind affirmed that being held was a mutually beneficial thing.

We retreated inside and shook off the chilly air. Sheba kept pace as I climbed the stairs and headed for the kitchen. I scanned the makeshift plywood shelving looking for her food. It was easy to spot because the kitchen was devoid of any furnishings. The cupboards, countertops, and appliances, though ordered, had yet to arrive.

I set the bowl of food on the dirty plywood subfloor. Sheba studied me before approaching her food. I slid to the floor with my back pressed against an unpainted wall.

"Eat up, girl, I'm not going anywhere today."

Satisfied I wasn't abandoning her, Sheba vacuumed up her food. It was almost time for our rendezvous with Patty. Sheba followed me into an adjacent room where I hid a shredded corduroy slipper. The unkept room would eventually become our living room, but for now it served as a supply depot. Sheba leaped for the slipper I held just out of reach. I lowered it enough for her to grab ahold of it and start a game of tug of war.

"Sheba, GIVE!"

We worked regularly on this command. She raised one eyebrow and then the other. The conflict in her mind was apparent. She wanted to please me, but she also had an intense desire for the slipper. My persistence eventually gave me the victory, and I rewarded her by flinging the slipper to the far corner of the room. Sheba dodged sawhorses and five-gallon buckets, scattered a swept-up pile of trash, and ducked under a ladder to grab her prize.

After a few more tosses, it was time to pick up Patty. Sheba abandoned the slipper only after she saw me move toward the door. She raced to keep up with me. Our return to the camper amounted to a family reunion as Sheba greeted Patty with the same enthusiasm I experienced less than an hour ago.

"I left the kerosene heater on, so we should get going."

"I'm ready," Patty replied.

Patty started a pot of coffee when we arrived at our partially built dwelling. Our Mr. Coffee coffeemaker was one of three identical units we received as wedding gifts, no doubt an indication of the similarities between our two families. I loved the aroma of coffee almost as much as the taste of it.

I grabbed a pair of clean putty knives and a bucket of drywall compound and went to work covering the joints and nail heads in our future bedroom with joint compound. The heater had done its job warming up the two rooms connected by a hallway. When Patty brought the coffee, it was a welcome relief to my hands and throat.

Everything I know about the drywalling process was taught to me by my father. Bill was slightly taller and quite a bit heavier than me. His most endearing quality besides wisdom was his patience. I may have acquired his knowledge, but only practice could raise my skill level. I wasn't an artist, but this seemed like something an artist would be good at. One's competence in seaming and sanding drywall was revealed after the walls were brandished with a coat of paint. Only then were the hidden mistakes exposed by the light like sins.

I placed two sawhorses end to end to make an extended platform to stand on. Much of the hard work had already been completed, but the ceiling work remained. I manipulated the mud back and forth between the two drywall knives. The sound likened itself to a pair of swordsmen locked in a duel. Once the mud, the consistency of mayonnaise, was in right position, I applied it directly overhead in one continuous motion. Blobs of compound routinely dripped off the edges of the blade as I spread it. The bill of my baseball cap saved me from getting a face full of white goop on multiple occasions.

While I worked, Patty cracked opened a textbook in the next room. Her mind engaged with the pool of medical knowledge that rested in her lap. Sheba snoozed at her feet in front of the kerosene heater. Sunlight flooded the room, illuminating thousands of suspended dust particles. A top-forty radio station droned on in the background, lessening the monotony of my travail.

Thoughts of Sheba entered my mind. I reflected on how tightly connected to her we'd become. Her devotion was unwavering. She had no bad days and concealed no deceit. I had become increasingly grounded just by being with her. Her love and devotion were emotional anchors. God knew what he was doing when He brought her into my life.

I continued working as the hands on my watch crept along. The sound of clicking toenails on the plywood floor grabbed my attention. Sheba appeared in the doorway with the tattered slipper in her mouth. Her head bobbed. Obviously, she wanted to play. I was ready for a much-needed break and another cup of coffee, so I hastily applied the remaining compound on my knife to an overhead seam and followed my progress with the second knife to smooth out any thick spots. Sheba's tail wagged when she saw me moving in her direction. She dropped the slipper on the floor and hovered over it.

A blob of mud fell from the ceiling when I wasn't expecting it, and I moved quickly to dodge it. Too quickly. My weight shifted, and I lost my balance. One foot caught nothing but air. I immediately realized there was nothing I could do to stop my fall. The sawhorse I was attempting to right myself on crashed on its side. I looked down in disbelief as my foot followed its unalterable course directly into the five-gallon bucket of drywall compound. My sneaker quickly disappeared into the white mud. It was an uncomfortably cool feeling to have drywall compound inch its way past my sneaker and sock and finally reach my bare skin.

"Patty, I need help!"

I heard her lawn chair scrape across the floor as she sprang to her feet. She rushed into the room, unsure what to expect.

"What's wrong?"

When she saw I was unharmed and standing with one foot in a bucket, she erupted with laughter. I stared back at her with a confused look on my face. Patty immediately ran out of the room and left me standing with my foot wedged in the bucket.

Embarrassed by my mishap and more than a little perturbed, I awkwardly tugged on my foot attempting to extract it. The mud emitted a sucking sound when it finally released its hold on my foot. My sneaker, sock and jeans would become plaster casts if they weren't rinsed off soon.

Patty returned with a camera in hand hoping to capture the moment on film. She pleaded with me to stick my foot back in the bucket. Reluctantly, I complied.

Patty and I were greatly encouraged by Sheba's arrival. Our puppy bathed us in devotion day after day. Devotion fosters encouragement, and with encouragement comes inspiration. I've heard it said that inspirational experiences can have a positive effect on one's belief in God, whether that inspiration comes from an awe-inspiring vista, or cradling a trembling puppy in your arms. The Christian experience relies heavily on daily devotion to God. How can we claim to know Him if we don't spend time with Him?

I was inspired by the fact that my relationship with Sheba brought no unknowns to be feared. She helped me see who I really was as a person, a husband, and not some scared young man trying to make the transition to adulthood. I was inspired by her to trust in the love of others. Religion, or an ideal, can't inspire devotion the way a relationship can. It wasn't until I prioritized my personal relationship with God that I began to appreciate God's love for me (John 3:16).

During this time, God was getting my attention. I could not deny His love for me nor His protection, though many times I felt as though I didn't deserve it. On several occasions during the construction of our house, I was spared severe injury or worse. On one of those occasions, I was standing on the top rung of a twenty-four-foot ladder when the top of the ladder moved a couple of inches away from the house. With both my hands already engaged at hammering a nail into the roof, I thought my end had come. After dropping my hammer and digging my fingernails into the shingles on the roof, I earnestly prayed for deliverance. I escaped injury when the ladder slapped back against the house. Moments later as I stood on the ground shaking, I knew God had spared my life. But for what purpose? For the first time, I wondered if there might be a divine plan for my life (Jeremiah 29:11). I felt closer to God that day. If Sheba's love was something I could depend on, how much more could I depend on God's love.

I was pushed back and about to fall, but the LORD helped me. The LORD is my strength and my defense; he has become my salvation.
(Psalm 118:13–14)

When I said, "My foot is slipping," your unfailing love, LORD, supported me. When anxiety was great within me, your consolation brought me joy. (Psalm 94:18–19)

There is no fear in love. But perfect love drives out fear. (1 John 4:18)

TWO

God Spelled Backward Is D-O-G

I JUMPED in my light blue Dodge pickup and tossed the bag of snacks I'd just purchased from the convenience store onto the seat next to me. If I hurried, I could beat the traffic light before it turned red. I revved the engine and backed out of the parking space. My tires chirped on the asphalt as I exited the parking lot. I quickly shifted into second gear and watched the light turn red in my rearview mirror. *That was close, but I made it!*

The tension in my arms waned as the road stretched out before me. I slid the floor-mounted stick shift into third gear and loosened my tight grip on the steering wheel. The chilled air spilling in through a gap in the window invigorated me.

I glanced in the side-view mirror, and a clean-shaven face with hazel eyes, short brown hair, and wire-rimmed glasses smiled back at me. When I saw there was no traffic in front of me, I realized I'd be home before halftime expired. *Life is good.*

I was a fan of Penn State football. Why, it's hard to say for certain. It likely had something to do with them winning the national championship back in 1982. Though I never played on a team in high school or college, I loved to watch the game. It fascinated me how each play began in such orderly fashion. I tensed along with the players as they waited for the snap of the ball. When it was hiked, order quickly turned into chaos. How many times have I neatly ordered my life only to watch some event turn everything to chaos? I often squirmed in my chair as I watched the ball carrier move down the field trying to avoid those who wanted to tackle him. Patty would tease me whenever she saw me squirming. She'd ask, "Are you trying to help the ball carrier?"

I reached over and rested a hand on my partner, Sheba, affirming her willingness to accompany me on the spur of the moment. My fingers tingled as I ran them through her hair. A distant siren was barely discernible above the sound of the air rushing in through the window. I saw no reason to pay attention to it.

I was having the best year of my life. At twenty-six, I was winning in so many areas. Patty graduated from college, and both of us now had full-time jobs. Our pinnacle achievement had to be moving into the house we'd labored for over a year to build.

When the curved highway straightened, I caught a glimpse of a squad car in my rearview mirror with its lights aglow. I glanced at my speedometer and confirmed I wasn't speeding. *Somebody's day is about to be ruined,* I thought. As the vehicle closed in on my rear bumper, I pulled off the highway to let it go by. But instead of sailing on past, the squad car pulled in tight behind me. I slammed both palms against the steering wheel.

"You've got to be kidding me!"

For several minutes the two of us sat in silence, waiting for the officer to emerge from his vehicle. Eventually, a stout man sporting mirrored sunglasses exited his vehicle and strutted toward us. He had a "don't mess with me" look about him. I let out a sigh and rolled down my window.

"Do you know why I pulled you over?" he asked.

"No sir, I don't," I said, remembering how my father always addressed uniformed personnel respectfully.

"Can I see your license and registration, please?"

I nervously gathered my information. When the officer reached through the open window to take possession of my documents, my one-year-old sidekick let out a growl. The sound caught me off guard and startled the officer. I'd never seen her react that way before. Sheba leaped in the direction of the officer. I wrapped my arms around her the moment she landed in my lap and pinned her body tight to my chest. Sheba had grown to more than sixty pounds, and when she voiced her concern, it left my ears ringing. While it was nice to have her on hand for support, any hope I had of getting out of this incident unscathed seemed to have gone out the window along with the officer.

"I clocked you doing fifty-five in a thirty-five-mile speed zone," the officer stated after regaining his composure.

"But this *is* a fifty-five-mile zone," I countered.

"Not back at the traffic light."

"Yes, I know that. There's a speed limit sign just past the intersection. I accelerated when I saw the sign."

He considered my explanation for a moment.

"All right . . . but you crossed a double yellow line going through the intersection."

My cheeks started to burn. *He is accusing me of something I don't think I did.* I was a little confused because the intersection was on a curve and there were no painted lines to cross. My mind whirled as I tried to come up with a viable response. How could he make this accusation unless he was following directly behind me? As far as I knew, I was the only vehicle on the highway. Surely, this guy had better things to do than harass me.

I pondered the situation further. *This must have something to do with me trying to beat the traffic light back at the intersection. He probably thinks I'm a reckless driver. How do I vindicate myself without calling him a liar?* My mind went blank, so I decided to say nothing.

I watched helplessly as the officer retreated to his patrol car. Immediately my thoughts turned heavenward. *Okay, God, what did I do to deserve this?* After a couple of minutes, I reconsidered the thought. *Why am I blaming God? Why is this suddenly His problem?*

"What do you think, Sheba?"

She looked up at me inquisitively when I mentioned her name. Her eyes conveyed complete devotion. There were times when I felt like I didn't deserve her love. This was one of them. A wave of conviction washed over me as I sat there looking for someone to blame for my troubles. How much did I really know about devotion? Was I as devoted to the people I cared about as Sheba was to me? Maybe a dog's devotion isn't a fair comparison.

I revisited a few recent successes intending for them to lift my spirits. The elation I experienced graduating from college, finishing the house, and winning a slow pitch softball championship all failed to lift me above my present circumstance.

A thought came into my head out of nowhere. *Is absolute devotion to success a form of idolatry? It seems like it could be, especially if I am withholding devotion from God.* My hyperactive mind made another leap. *Is misplacing my devotion akin to being unfaithful?* The thought of being unfaithful made me feel dirty, so I cast aside the thought and tried to focus on the current situation I found myself in.

I continued to stoke Sheba's fur, which gave my idle hands something to do while I waited. My eyes found comfort in her beauty.

"You love me, don't you, girl?" I said, giving her neck a big hug.

The sheriff tapped on the partially open window, startling me. He returned my papers to me while keeping a wary eye on Sheba. A bright yellow traffic ticket rested on top of the pile. Sheba glared at him and growled. The thought of having to pay a fine for something I was convinced I didn't do soured my mood.

In a departure from my character, I exchanged no further pleasantries. Instead, I hastily rolled up the window as if the act would somehow make the whole incident go away. It didn't help. I scanned the road in both directions and pulled back onto the highway. It was then I noticed how close I was to home.

"If any of my neighbors are watching, they'll certainly want to know why I was pulled over by the police," I complained to my canine companion.

Sheba whined, sensing my frustration, and walked the length of the bench seat, repositioning herself by the passenger door.

I pulled into my driveway, and the football game I'd rushed home to watch no longer held my interest. Patty was working, so only Sheba was there to console me. My bad news would have to wait. I set the ticket on the kitchen table and vowed to forget about it for a while. I turned my attention to Sheba, believing she could brighten my day.

"Where's the bunny rabbit?"

Sheba's head shot up from between her paws. She understood the words. I repeated them just to watch her animated response. It felt good to laugh.

She sprang to her feet, ran to the window, and rested both front paws on the sill. From her vantage point, one and a half stories above the ground, she could survey the entire backyard. Her initial bark was one of anticipation.

Her wet nose made streaks across the window as her hot breath fogged the glass. When her barks suddenly turned aggressive, I knew she spotted something. She clawed at the glass and the wooden sill. I had precious little time to act before her actions became destructive.

I opened the kitchen door and yelled above the barking, "Sheba! Go get the bunny rabbit!"

She rocketed through the doorway. It was pointless for me to try and keep pace. I grabbed the softball bat I kept behind the door and casually made my exit.

Sheba hurled herself down the steps affixed to the side of the house and made a sharp U-turn onto the driveway, spraying gravel against the siding. Without hesitation, she glided down an eight-foot embankment and entered the backyard on a dead run. I smiled when I caught her glancing over her shoulder to see if I was following her. Sheba was aware of the bat in my hand, but she hadn't forgotten about the rabbit either.

I knew very little about rabbit behavior but considered it strange that they didn't flee the moment they sensed danger. The rabbit certainly heard Sheba bearing down on it. Yet it wasn't until the last possible moment that the creature bolted in the direction of the cow pasture adjoining our property.

Despite being on a dead run, Sheba didn't catch the rabbit. I witnessed this scenario on a regular basis. Like an Olympic athlete, the rabbit sprinted across the finish line, a five-foot-high wire fence with six-by-eight-inch openings. The victor paused to graze on tender shoots of grass in plain sight of the loser. Sheba couldn't see the humor in it. She barked incessantly as drool dripped from her jaws.

"You'll get the bunny next time," I yelled.

Sheba's nonstop barking annoyed the rabbit to the point that it finally loped away. Ironically, the rabbit's brush with danger wouldn't deter its behavior. We'd probably spot it in our backyard in a couple of days.

Sheba continued to stare into the pasture hoping the bunny would return. A pair of black-and-white cows moseyed over to see what all the fuss was about. By the time they arrived, the drama had played itself out. The presence of the cows didn't seem to bother Sheba. They were more like neighbors than interlopers.

I stood in the basement doorway, gripping an aluminum bat in one hand and a well-worn softball in the other. I banged my war club on the concrete patio and waited for Sheba to look in my direction.

The temperature was falling. I shook off the chill that ran up my back. Sheba stood motionless, staring at me. Her eyes were trained on the objects I held like a pointer waiting for the command to flush a gamebird out of hiding. Water vapor trailed from her mouth as she panted. Her leg muscles twitched as she awaited my next move. I tossed the ball in the air to offer her a glimpse of the prize. The drool dripping out of the corners of her mouth betrayed her desire for it. Finally, when she couldn't take the wait any longer, she launched herself toward me in what could only be described as an enthusiastic rage.

The game we were about to play rivaled her love for chasing rabbits. I would throw the ball, and she would retrieve it. The bat became part of the game when I got tired of straining the muscles in my throwing arm. The sound of the bat colliding with the ball seemed to drive her crazy. You could say we felt the same way about those annoying squeaky toys she ripped to shreds as a puppy.

Sheba's reckless charge abruptly ended when I struck the ball with the bat. She hit the brakes and searched for the ball in the sky. The moment she spotted the ball making its gentle arc across the faded blue sky, she immediately gave chase. Unlike an outfielder, Sheba was not worried about catching the ball before it hit the ground. Her satisfaction came from retrieving it.

The ball landed in a soggy patch at the back edge of our property. Because I didn't see it bounce, I figured it had gotten stuck in the mud. Undeterred, Sheba maintained her sprint. Her nose guided her to the ball. I laughed when I saw her theatrical pounce.

Sheba returned with the ball and dropped it on the ground between her front feet just out of my reach. This was a game she liked to play. She looked up at me, then down at the ball, daring me to grab it. If I lunged for it too quickly, she'd collapse on it and growl. I played along and made several halfhearted attempts just to watch her zealously guard her prize.

"Well, do you want me to hit the ball again or not?"

I feigned boredom and turned my back on her. My disinterest caused her great concern. She left the ball unguarded and circled around in front of me to see if I was okay. I peeked over my shoulder trying to determine the perfect moment to snatch the ball.

The moment I took possession, a fiery determination returned to her eyes. She bounced with joy knowing our game would continue, barking to exhort me on.

I batted the ball again. This time I connected squarely with the ball and sent it soaring more than two hundred feet. It carried well beyond the back of our property and was swallowed up by the swamp. If I was playing with anyone else, it would be game over because the ball would be lost in the cattails. I dropped the bat, raised both hands in the air, and launched into a homerun trot circling imaginary bases. Sheba charged headlong into the cattails. This was a challenge she lived for. I was confident she'd find the ball because she hadn't disappointed me yet.

Beyond the swamp, the woodlands offered a delightful view. It was the sort of image that found its way onto artists' canvases. The hardwood trees were adorned with yellow, red, and orange leaves and were punctuated every so often by blue and green evergreens. The intensity of the color was magnified by the sun's low angle and the approaching dark clouds.

I've been awed by this type of scenery since I was a teen. Wooded areas have always held a timeless mystique about them. Back then I tried to imagine what it would be like living in colonial times and spotting Native Americans in their native habitat. I'd sit for hours listening to the song of the leaves rustling in the wind. When I returned to the woods as winter approached, the trees were naked. I'd shuffle through the whispering blanket of leaves on the ground with the same reverence as someone wandering through a cemetery.

Trees were not the only thing I observed in the woods. I remember watching creatures carrying out their fall agendas. For these creatures, time was of the essence. They spent the precious little time they did have before winter hoarding and gorging themselves on whatever food was available. If death came for them, it wasn't just for a season, like with the trees. I concluded a creature's life was not that different from humans. We all seemed to live a life of extremes, whether it be a life of excess or depravity.

Sheba emerged from the swamp and shook out her coat. Water dripped from the fur around her belly as she trotted back to me. With her head held high she mouthed her muddy prize. She flicked the ball out of her mouth and sent it rolling toward my feet.

"What, no keep-away this time?"

She lobbied to keep the game going by spinning in circles and jumping high into the air. I knew she longed for another plunge into the swamp. I squatted low to the ground and moved toward the ball in slow motion. The delay drove her crazy. Sheba changed her mind and lunged for the ball. We reached it at the same time, and the collision sent me tumbling over backward.

I laughed loudly as I lay on the ground and stared up at the sky. Laughing reminded me of how precious and fulfilling life could be. I curled up and hid the ball from Sheba. She countered by probing my body with her nose in search of the softball. I squirmed and repositioned it several times to keep it concealed. She burrowed through my defenses and snorted in my face. When she couldn't find the ball, she became flustered, backed away, and started barking.

I honored Sheba by continuing our game. A few batted balls found their way into the swamp, but most fell short. Regardless of how far the ball traveled, she retrieved each one with the same measure of enthusiasm. Her attitude toward our game—toward me— led me to believe I was highly esteemed. It became clear that all Sheba really wanted was to spend time with me.

The dark clouds were almost over us. The light breeze we were contending with had stiffened, driving the temperature downward. A particularly strong gust sent a platoon of leaves tumbling across the ground until they fortified their position behind tall tufts of grass. The wind brought with it the faint smell of rain.

Sheba followed me through the back door still gripping the soggy ball in her jaws. I dried her off with an old towel. Loving the attention, she flipped over on her back so I could rub down her belly. Her feet paddled the air while I rubbed.

"Let's get a fire going," I said, injecting enthusiasm into my voice.

The positive inflection in my voice sent her tail wagging. I felt her thick tail whack my pant leg repeatedly while I mopped up the wet mess we made. I whipped the towel around on the floor while Sheba, believing this to be another game, made several attempts to grab it.

We circled around to the other side of the stairs which served to divide the basement in half. Most of the basements I've been in were dreary places, but ours offered a special attraction—a wood-burning stove flanked by a pair of rocking chairs.

Like a good Boy Scout, I busied myself shaping a few pieces of kindling into a teepee. I stuffed wadded-up newspaper into the formation and set it ablaze using a single match. Sheba plopped down beside me and placed her chin on my calf. She looked on nervously when her nose picked up the scent of smoke. I fanned the smoldering wood until it burst into a healthy flame. After the chimney warmed, it began to draw away the smoke.

"See, it's okay, girl."

I patted her on the head, and she responded with a yawn. The orange flames surged, and the wood crackled. I fed the hungry blaze a couple more pieces of wood. When I was satisfied the fire wouldn't die out, I shoved a large chunk of cordwood into the firebox and closed the cast iron doors.

I loved the roaring sound air made when it was sucked in through the stove vents. In a matter of minutes, the warmth radiating from the stove reached me. I sank into a chair, giving my body a chance to liberate itself from the weight of the day. The rhythmic creaking of the rocking chair had a soothing effect on my mind.

I watched slivers of light bleed out through the stove vents and dance on the floor. Peace rose within me like cream in an undisturbed pail of milk. I felt my thoughts begin to drift.

I glanced down at the crooked finger on my left hand and remembered . . . *high school . . . senior year . . . the feeling I finally belonged . . . skipping study hall to play team handball . . . wrong place, wrong time . . . a broken finger for the rest of my life.*

My eyes traveled to the scar on my right thumb . . . *college . . . my junior year . . . I loved being on my own . . . throwing caution to the wind . . . horsing around with my roommate . . . I attempted to save a falling mirror . . . a gash . . . my roommate almost passed out at the sight . . . stitches . . . scarred for the rest of my life.*

I spun the wedding ring on my finger, the only piece of jewelry I wore besides my watch . . . *senior year in college . . . swept off my feet by a freshman . . . experiencing love I never knew before . . . my proposal . . . how a simple "yes" changed my life forever.*

Sheba's damp fur touched my legs. I knew I wasn't the only

person carrying scars and symbols through life. But I saw God in all of them. He was there in the bad times when I prayed as well as the good times when I was having fun. Without His hand on my life, I doubted I would have ever met Patty. I paused to thank God for her.

~

I spent time by the fire dwelling on God's goodness and His faithfulness to me. Sheba was a product of that goodness. I realized she was purposefully made, a creature that engaged me personally, just like I tried to do with God. She served as an everyday reminder of what love and faithfulness looked like. I realized it probably wasn't a coincidence God spelled backward was D-O-G. It seemed to me that the destinies of humans and dogs were intentionally linked. Did the two creatures exist to serve one another?

Because I regarded the Bible as truth, I was curious about what it had to say about dogs. From the creation account in Genesis 1, I knew dogs were pronounced "good" on the sixth day. I also knew they were among the animals preserved through the flood of Noah's day. But something happened to their reputation when they were left to run wild with others of their own kind. Scripture portrays these rogue dogs as dangerous, carnivorous, vile, and deplorable. Adding to their already tarnished reputation, they were used as idioms for morally and spiritually depraved men. If someone in ancient times called you a "dog," it meant you were a despicable person. It was the worst insult someone could give.

Today we see dogs as benevolent creatures. What led to their transformation? You could say the answer lies in some kind of redemption; a spiritual connection brought about by a personal relationship with humans. Is God trying to teach us something by using such a lowly creature to influence our lives? Perhaps God is telling us we are not God, and without a personal relationship with Him we cannot be rescued. If left to our own devices, we will become spiritually and morally depraved men and women.

For the foolishness of God is wiser than human wisdom, and the weakness of God is stronger than human strength. . . But God chose the foolish things of the world to shame the wise; God chose the weak things of the world to shame the strong. (1 Corinthians 1:25–27)

And you . . . serve him [God] with wholehearted devotion and with a willing mind, for the LORD searches every heart and understands every desire and every thought. If you seek him, he will be found by you. (1 Chronicles 28:9)

Take delight in the LORD, and he will give you the desires of your heart. (Psalm 37:4)

THREE

A Child Changes Everything

THE AFTERNOON SUN beat down on me, burning my flesh. The T-shirt I wore was soaked with sweat and clung to me when I moved. Perspiration trickled down my arms and drizzled into the leather work gloves I wore. My hands slipped inside the gloves as I struggled to maintain my grip on a sixteen-pound wood-splitting maul. I hoisted the bright orange maul above my head and enlisted the aid of gravity to force it down. The tool vibrated in my hands when it came to an abrupt stop but not before creating an ugly fissure in an eighteen-inch-thick section of log. I wrestled the maul free.

Sheba, now two years old, looked on from a safe distance tethered to her dog run like an unwilling soul bound to an illness. Given a choice, I'd have let her run around the yard, but it was too risky while I swung the maul. I raised the tool a second time and finished the task, cleaving the block of wood in two.

I've been told firewood heats twice. Body heat is generated when wood is chopped into pieces. The wood gives off heat a second time when it's burned in a stove. I've also been told if you want to save money, buy a truck load of logs, and split the wood yourself. Since I didn't have experience using a chain saw, I purchased logs already cut into blocks. When the wood arrived, I lined eight shipping pallets across the center of our backyard intending to use them to stack two rows of firewood chest high. I'd almost competed the back row, but the front section was nearly empty.

I wiped the sweat off my face using my shirt. My aching limbs gave me a fresh perspective on the romantic notion of relaxing beside a crackling fire. Today I wished I was completely enveloped by winter's chill. At least then I could have put the heat generated by my body to good use.

The baseball cap I wore kept the sweat from irritating my eyes, but it also collected heat from my scalp. I ventured over to the spigot at the back of the house and doused my head with cold water. Sheba lifted her head off her paws just long enough to see what I was doing. For the time being, she was content to relax in a shady spot under the only tree on our property. I quenched my thirst and returned to the task at hand.

I carried one of the smaller log sections over to my work area. I didn't have to remind myself I had a wife and baby to support. How was it possible that Patty and I had reached the threshold of our dreams so quickly? Like many married couples our age, success came at a high price: a mortgage, credit card bills, student loan debt, and a car payment. None of that mattered to me before. Yesterday, however, my employment status entered the realm of uncertainty, and the debt we had hanging over us had suddenly become a noose. I sliced through the section of log with a single blow.

It surprised me how the birth of our first child completely changed my approach to life; how I drove, what I purchased, how I spent my time, the sudden interest in improving my status at work, you name it—it all changed. Two more blows fractured the split log into manageable pieces. We were meeting our financial obligations because both of us had full-time jobs. I took our paychecks for granted and believed they'd always be there. It was unsettling to know the world owed us nothing.

There were sharp bends and dangerous obstacles hiding beneath the surface of the river of life. Patty and I were not looking far enough ahead to avoid them. Now a stretch of rough water threatened to ruin us. The worrywart in me should have been raising caution flags along the way. I guess I'd fallen in love with the ease at which we were accomplishing our goals. Because we were so blessed, I started to believe bad things wouldn't happen to us.

I rolled a large block into position and tipped it on end, exposing its face. The process was simple enough. Batter the block of wood until it broke into manageable pieces. The pieces conformed to their intended purpose and became a burden more easily managed. Can't life's problems be solved in the same manner? If so, I wondered what "the battering" would cost us.

My mind replayed the words *Our company is downsizing.* Yesterday's meeting with Lee, my supervisor, and John, the company's newly appointed vice president, had come without warning. During the meeting, I struggled to keep pace with what was being said. John used the word *downsizing* as if it were a piece of trash that could easily be dealt with. Why was I the one sitting there? I had done everything they ever asked of me. My performance reviews reflected that. I found it odd that Lee sat stoically beside me and only offered an occasional nod. It dawned on me the two of them were already on the same page.

I forced myself to listen, fighting to keep panic from usurping my thoughts. Was this going to be the end of everything Patty and I had worked for? The timing couldn't have been worse—Patty and I had a child to support.

"We'd like to keep you on as an employee and make you assistant supervisor," John said. That sounded like good news. I liked Lee, and now I was going to be his assistant. If this was good news, why weren't they weren't smiling? It became clear when he added, "You'll have to switch to the graveyard shift," (eleven p.m. to seven a.m.). I loved working days. Suddenly, this seemed more like a punishment. I was finding it difficult to keep my mind from shutting down. When I asked if there would be a pay increase, he answered no because our company was having financial difficulties.

Under a different set of circumstances this would have been a promotion. Maybe that's how they saw it. I'd graduate from filling the molding machines with plastic pellets to helping the supervisor answer trouble lights and horns, mechanisms the operators used to call for help when the machines malfunctioned. But because there would be fewer machines running, I was expected to do my current job *and* be the assistant supervisor for the same pay.

I asked about Roger whose place I'd be taking on the graveyard shift. I was told not to concern myself with him. I realized how serious the situation was, and it scared me. Roger was a good friend of mine. My mind began filling in the blank spaces where the information was missing. The conversation ended abruptly after I was told, "If you'd rather not take this position, we'd be happy to supply you with a good job reference."

I'd worked the graveyard shift before as a machine operator while on college break. I didn't like the hours. By three o'clock in the morning, my body begged for sleep. The repetitive rhythm of the molding machine made it almost impossible to stay awake. If I remember right, that was the summer I started drinking coffee because I had so much trouble staying awake. *This would be different,* I told myself. *I'll try to keep an open mind until I talk to Patty.*

I couldn't chop wood any longer. Pushing myself to the brink of physical exhaustion was not the answer. Interrogating my thoughts didn't bring any revelation either. I picked up the pieces of wood littering the ground and stacked them on the woodpile.

Sheba gathered herself into a sitting position when she noticed my work pattern had changed. What began with a whine morphed into woofs when she realized she wasn't getting my attention. She began to bark when I made my way toward her.

I set her free and watched the anxiety melt off her faster than butter heated in a pan. The joy she exhibited lifted my spirit and convinced me that I should let go of my worries for the time being. Sheba trotted around the woodpile as if inspecting my work. The exercise helped loosen her stiff limbs. Her tail whirled in a circle and reminded me of a helicopter rotor. What was the secret to her joy?

Sheba's nose picked up a familiar scent. Immediately, she became obsessed with finding it. Her nose explored every nook and cranny in the woodpile. She glanced frequently in my direction as if asking for my help. I knew what she was looking for because I'd hidden the object in the woodpile yesterday. Moments later her nose verified what her eyes couldn't see. Sheba raced back and forth between the woodpile and me. I took my time getting there because I knew the wait would heighten her excitement.

The crazed creature I called Sheba became hyperactive when I uncovered a carefully hidden Frisbee. She threw her body in tight circles and barked nonstop. The sun's blistering rays warmed the disc as I held it. I made a mental note not to overextend my companion.

I held the Frisbee over Sheba's head. She seated herself like a statue and stared at it intensely. Drool seeped out of the corners of her mouth. I waved the Frisbee around, knowing it would drive her crazy. When she couldn't take the wait any longer, she launched herself vertically and snatched it out of my hand. Fortunately, my fingers remained clear of her teeth.

"Sheba, give!"

Reluctantly, she complied. It wasn't that long ago Sheba and I had started playing with a Frisbee. She had destroyed the softballs we used to play with one at a time. She took a liking to chewing the leather covers off them when I wasn't looking. What possesses someone to hurt an object they love instead of nurturing and cherishing it? In Sheba's case, she may have felt neglected. When Dan was born, he was the recipient of a lot of love. Sheba wasn't used to sharing the affection she received.

Sheba's approach to retrieving a Frisbee was no different from fetching a softball, that is, until the day she managed to catch the orange disc midflight. From that moment on she became obsessed with grabbing it before it hit the ground. She became so good at catching a Frisbee that onlookers thought she was trying to show off.

She dug her claws into the parched ground, sprinting in the direction she thought I'd throw the Frisbee before it left my hand. I flung it and watched it glide four feet above the ground on a low, flat trajectory. Sheba found another gear when the Frisbee sailed past her. Her body moved like an arrow launched from a bow. She reached it just as it began its descent. I felt I'd done my part when her jaws successfully clamped down on it. It was a thing of beauty watching her muscles ripple beneath her glossy black coat. It was hard not to see that this was something she was born to do. I caught myself wondering, *What was it I was put on this earth to do?*

She dropped the Frisbee at my feet. I reached for it cautiously. On more than one occasion Sheba had accidentally bitten my fingers when we grabbed for it at the same time. I scooped up the Frisbee and hurried another throw. The disc rose like an airplane during takeoff and stalled in the middle of its climb. Sheba, already waiting beneath it, watched it drop out of the sky. A perfectly timed leap, her nose reaching more than six feet off the ground, resulted in another spectacular catch. She seemed pleased with herself and trotted back to me with her head held high, waving her prize in the air.

I could see Sheba was overheating after a few more tosses. Her tongue hung out of the side of her mouth while her sides heaved in and out. She didn't want to quit. I marveled at her determination and could tell by her body language she didn't understand why we were stopping. I carried the Frisbee indoors knowing she would follow.

As dinner wound down, I launched into the dreaded conversation I had put off for as long as I could. Thinking about my job soured the food I forced myself to eat. I hoped Patty could provide me some much-needed clarity.

"What do you think I should do about work?" I asked. "It doesn't feel right accepting this job at Roger's expense."

"You're not the one taking away his job," Patty replied. "And don't underestimate your ability, Bill. You might be a better fit for what they have planned in the future."

"I got the impression he'd be laid off, although they didn't come right out and say it."

"Are you worried he'll hold a grudge against you?"

"Yes, I love playing softball with him. He's an amazing player to watch. I don't want him to quit the team because I'm the coach. I guess it's going to be one of those times I'll be forced to lean heavily on God."

"You use the word *forced* like this is God's doing. You know that's not the case. We could both stand to rely on Him more."

"I didn't mean it quite like that."

"While we're on the subject of work, we need to talk about my job."

"Oh no! What's happened?"

"Nothing happened yet. It's just that ever since I returned to work, all I can think about is how much I miss being home with Dan. I can't bear the thought of somebody else raising our son."

Her disclosure broke the dam of tears she'd been holding back. My stomach churned as I felt walls of uncertainty closing in on us from every direction. I guess I couldn't blame Patty for wanting to be home as much as possible with our son. The timing couldn't have been worse, however. What would our future look like if we both changed jobs or schedules?

At that moment I didn't feel strong or brave. How was I going to assure her everything would be all right? What could I do to ease our burdens? It was pointless to push the conversation any further without processing what had already been said. We struggled to our feet, fell into each other's arms, and melted in a pool of tears. A wave of helplessness overtook me. Whatever happened next was liable to change our lives forever.

Dan looked on from his high chair. He didn't understand why we were sad, but he knew he was being ignored. The sound of his tiny hands banging on the high chair tray grabbed our attention. Apparently, he'd had enough of pinching Cheerios with his fingers and stuffing them in his mouth. He wanted in on some of the attention Patty and I were giving each other.

I lifted Dan out of his chair and headed down to the basement where I knew it would be cooler. Air-conditioning was a luxury we couldn't afford. Perhaps a change of scenery would shed new light on things.

Sheba followed me down the stairs. The air in the basement was noticeably cooler and carried the faint smell of new carpet. I dug my toes into the raised pile.

Half of the basement had undergone a transformation while I waited for Dan to be born. I'd created a family room by adding drywall, carpeting, and a suspended ceiling. I was so proud of my first home improvement effort, a product of all the knowledge I'd accumulated. Patty had injected her ideas into the room, which included adding a pair of closets flanking an existing window. I also added a window seat for her to sit on so she could keep track of our children when they were old enough to play in the backyard.

The joy I normally felt when I entered the space suddenly felt tainted. Perhaps it was a poor financial decision to renovate the basement, considering our present circumstances.

I set Dan on the carpet and stretched out beside him. Sheba wedged her way in between us and leaned against me. Dan extended a tiny hand toward her ear. Sheba, knowing how precious the child was to us, posed like the Sphinx, allowing him to touch her. I could see the two of them becoming best friends someday. I pulled one of Dan's toys closer so he could play with it.

I resisted the temptation to embrace regret. Instead, I dwelled on Patty and my storybook life thus far. We were truly blessed with jobs, a house, a child, and Sheba. We'd achieved everything we set out to do. I wondered how I'd react if some of it were taken away? Would I still feel blessed?

I had a radical thought. Were Patty and I being guided by God? I couldn't think of a good reason at first. Deep down inside me, a possibility emerged. Were we at a crossroad that called for a choice to be made? I couldn't deny that I was clinging to the house. It was my most prized possession. I believed it defined who I was. What would happen if I let go of it for the sake of my family? I tried to figure out why I was holding on to it so tightly. Perhaps too many dreams were still locked in its closets.

I gave myself permission to consider the possibility of letting go of it. Part of me resisted. Wouldn't surrendering the house amount to a failure on my part? My inner spirit decided the answer was no. If God's plan included reordering our priorities, then following Him would be an act of obedience, not failure. Was I willing to trust God with our future no matter what it looked like?

I rubbed Sheba's back. She raised her head and looked at me. It's hard to believe that two years prior we had just been getting acquainted. I thought she would want me to do the right thing. That meant working midnights to support my family. Patty was right: I should embrace this uncertainty as an opportunity and forge ahead. If the job didn't work out, I could always find another one. If Patty got her wish to work part-time, the house would have to go. I guess we really were at a crossroad.

The sound of dishes being cleaned by hand drifted down the stairs. No matter what happened, Patty and I still had each other. I can remember telling God after I fell in love with her, "She's all I ever wanted or needed." I watched Dan as he gripped a brightly colored plastic ring with both hands. He mustered all the coordination he possessed, attempting to place the yellow ring on a rocking spire. I recalled the joy we felt when he first came into our lives.

My mind continued to spin scenarios, wondering if I had overlooked something. I knew the exercise would be futile. There were too many unknowns. I decided to spend time affirming my relationship with God instead. I needed him to be my North Star. He would be my tour guide into the unknown. I couldn't journey on without this reference point.

A tiny hand pressed against my arm. *Yes, Lord, a child changes everything.* I remembered in that moment how many times we'd asked God to bless us with one.

I pulled Dan to my chest and bench-pressed him slowly, rocking him gently from side to side as I raised my arms up and down. He giggled with delight. The creaking stairs caught my attention. Patty lowered herself on the carpet behind me, tickling Dan's feet as I continued to play with him. I felt the warmth of her breath on my neck and the softness of her hand on my chest.

"We're going to have to make some drastic changes if you're serious about working part-time," I said quietly. "We're barely making ends meet as it is."

"Yes, I'm serious," she said, whispering in my ear.

"Even if that means selling the house?"

"If it means I can stay home with Dan, we should sell it."

"This is hard. We built this place. We *are* the story these walls would tell if they could talk. I know your dad will be disappointed. He built this for you."

"He built it for *us*," Patty said, correcting me. "I'll talk to my father. If we're both okay with selling it, isn't that all that really matters?"

Silence settled over the room. Both our minds were busy processing a possibility we'd once thought unthinkable.

Patty ran her fingers through my hair. "Just know that no matter what happens, you're the man I love. God gave *you* to me, and he gave *us* this beautiful child. He's not going to abandon us after all He's done."

I felt like I needed to pray. "God, we need your help figuring this out. We know how much you care about us. Please show us what to do. If that means selling the house, please send us a buyer. I've done a lousy job with our finances, and we need your help to make this work. Please open and shut doors as you see fit. We acknowledge everything we have is because of your goodness to us. We ask these things in Jesus's name. Amen."

Patty added a decisive "Amen."

I took the job on the graveyard shift but avoided my new supervisor as much as possible because I believed him to be a tyrant. He carried himself like a greaser straight out of *Happy Days*: white T-shirt and slicked-back black hair. One day, with a cigarette hanging out of his mouth, he asked, "Why do you keep avoiding me?" We talked at length, and he put my fears to rest. I hated the hours I was working, but I proved to be a capable assistant.

Our house went up for sale after we had difficult conversations with both sets of our parents, who were so involved in building it. I couldn't escape feeling I had failed them. I wondered if they thought I'd taken the easy way out. Not only was this experience humbling, but embarrassment, real or imagined, dogged me whenever I spent time with family.

We continued praying for a buyer and a good offer. If we were giving up the house, we needed to recoup as much money as possible. On the advice of our realtor, we added a third bedroom in the unused attic space at the top of the stairs. This decision increased our debt load, but it also allowed us to bump up our asking price and broadened the pool of potential buyers.

We felt vulnerable through the whole process, like an artist attempting to justify his or her asking price for one of their paintings. I knew God was with us, and I talked to Him more than ever.

Jesus said to Simon Peter, "Simon son of John, do you love me more than these [the reader can insert any type of hindrance]?" "Yes, Lord," he said, "you know that I love you." (John 21:15)

Therefore . . . let us throw off everything that hinders and the sin that so easily entangles. And let us run with perseverance the race marked out for us. (Hebrews 12:1)

And we know that in all things God works for the good of those who love him, who have been called according to his purpose. (Romans 8:28)

FOUR

The Ultimate Sacrifice

SUNLIGHT PEAKED in through a slit in the bedroom curtains striking my face like the beam of a flashlight. Our house was uncomfortably warm at this early hour. The portable fan we used to move the air around did nothing to quell the humidity. I sank lower in the cool water bed sheets, enamored with the notion of going back to sleep. A faint gibberish drifted into the room distinct from the sound of the whirling fan blades. I sighed. Though my heart welcomed the innocent sounds, my body lobbied for more sleep. I resigned myself to tend to Dan.

Gentle waves moved back and forth over the surface of the water bed mattress as I rolled up on my side. The movement pushed Sheba up against my legs. She was very possessive of the bottom corner of our bed and growled at me when I nudged her. Patty was still asleep, bobbing on the ripples.

"Sheba, move," I whispered as loud as I dared.

She growled again expressing her displeasure. Then, because of my persistence, she leaped out of bed, creating a violent wave that jolted Patty awake.

"Good morning, dear," she said, shaking the sleepiness from her voice.

"Sorry we woke you up."

"It's probably time to feed Dan anyway."

"I'll go get him for you."

Bringing a child into this world had eclipsed all my experiences to date. It amazed me that Patty and I had created another human being. Fatherhood, I discovered, was a mixed blessing. Many exciting things can happen while rearing a child, but sacrifices also need to be made. Sheba seemed aware of that. Ever since Dan came home from the hospital, she shadowed me closer than ever. The tiny human had diverted much of our attention away from her. This caused Sheba to vie for our attention in unusual ways.

A few days prior, she had chewed off the corner of one of Dan's storybooks. It was so out of character for her to do such a thing. I couldn't help but wonder if she was sending us a message. Patty and I were trying our best to keep things as normal as possible despite the "For Sale" sign in the front yard.

Dan sat in his crib conversing with a chestnut-colored teddy bear that was almost as big as he was. He'd gotten quite mobile recently, and his vocabulary was beginning to bloom. From a distance I watched his tiny fingers explore the bear's face and ears. It felt like I was catching a glimpse of his personality as I watched him talk to the bear.

Patty was content to have a sparsely decorated nursery. Besides the crib, there was a white dresser, which doubled as a changing table, and a rocking chair. She placed a latch-hook rug bearing the image of a teddy bear, which we'd made ourselves, in front of the crib. I hung a large handmade quilt on the wall opposite the crib. Patty selected bright yellow paint, which gave the room a peaceful glow when the afternoon sun bathed the room with light.

"Hi, Dan."

"Dad-dee!" he said, clutching the bear by the ear.

"Come see Daddy."

He wobbled to a standing position by hugging the rail of the crib and said, "Up."

Flailing arms expressed a joy his limited vocabulary could not. I turned my head from side to side trying to prevent him from grabbing my glasses, but this became a game to him.

Patty would notice the odor coming from his diaper. We had an agreement that after Dan was born, "If you're holding the baby and you smell something, you're the one who has to take care of it." I guess you could call that the number two rule. Sheba took an interest in the ripe smell filling the room and put her front paws on the dresser hoping to get a closer look.

"Down, girl."

I mentally prepared myself for what I was about to witness before I peeled back the cloth diaper. From experience I knew the mess could easily spread if I wasn't fully awake when taking on this task. My motto became "Brace for the worst and celebrate anything less."

I finished the procedure and placed Dan in Patty's arms. Sheba remained close to me while I dressed. Her tail started wagging the moment I reached for my shoes. For some reason she equated shoes with playtime. Regardless of what I intended to do next, Sheba hoped it involved her. If I had a tail, however, I wouldn't be wagging it until I finished dealing with the dirty diaper on the changing table.

I entered the bathroom carrying the soiled diaper by its corners. Sheba trotted beside me mouthing a yellow tennis ball she'd found somewhere in the house. It was a welcome relief when the lump of poo separated cleanly from the diaper without needing to rinse the cloth. Drawn by the fragrance, Sheba crowded the bowl. I flushed the toilet and lifted the lid on the diaper pail we kept near the toilet for soiled diapers. When I spun back around to put the toilet seat down (rule number one), the yellow ball disappeared down the toilet.

"What did you do?" I shouted.

Sheba hurried out of the room and went to find Patty. She had a habit of doing this whenever I scolded her. I flushed the toilet a couple of times hoping the ball would follow the poop and disappear. Each time I flushed the water rose to the rim and retreated very slowly indicating a blockage.

"I can't believe that just happened," I barked.

From down the hall Patty responded, "*What* just happened?"

"Sheba dropped a tennis ball into the toilet while I was flushing it. Now the toilet is plugged."

Seconds later Patty appeared in the doorway holding Dan. "Seriously?"

With great difficulty I managed a smile. "Someday we'll have a good laugh about this, but right now I'm too discouraged. I need to take apart the toilet."

Sheba was concerned about my sour mood and peaked in on me several times while I labored. I drained the toilet as best as I could and disconnected it from the plumbing. With the back of the toilet still attached, I carefully flipped the whole thing end over end. The remaining water spilled on to the floor, but to my amazement the ball also fell out. Sheba lunged for it as if it were part of a game.

"Oh, no you don't," I said, snatching it up and carrying it over to the sink.

I returned to my tools, and my unexpected success caused my frustration to melt away. How often was I able to fix a problem without any complications? Sheba, sensing my mood had changed, wouldn't stop hounding me. As I worked to reattach the plumbing, I fended her off with my elbow. She kept trying to wedge her head under my arm because she wanted to lick my face. That was not going to happen, knowing where her tongue had been. I was determined to stay clear of it.

"Sorry I yelled at you," I said. "Please don't ever do that again."

When our house first went on the market, many people toured it but very few showed interest. The continuous parade of people through our home served as a painful reminder that one day this place would be torn from our grasp. We were extremely disappointed that we still hadn't received an offer in the two months we had it listed. We had reached the point where I just wanted to get the whole thing over with.

Sheba didn't like strangers walking through the house, especially when Dan was there. She may have been disappointed in the attention she received from us, but she was zealous about protecting Dan from strangers. One morning she expressed her displeasure in a most unusual way.

Habitually, we accepted every request to show the house because we thought if enough people saw the house, eventually we would get an offer. Buyers were being very selective, however. I agreed to a tour on a Saturday morning at eight a.m., which I probably shouldn't have done. Patty was working, so I had precious little time to get the house ready. I walked in the kitchen door after working all night, paid the babysitter, tidied up the main floor, and got Dan up and dressed before the realtor arrived with her clients. I held Dan in my arms and tried to keep Sheba calm while the prospective buyers walked through the house.

The tour eventually made its way to the basement where I relished the opportunity to show off my proudest achievement—the family room. While I was talking, my gaze fell upon a large steaming pile of dog poo in the middle of the room. I was embarrassed beyond words. What else could I do but pretend it wasn't there and continue with the tour. I guess I wasn't surprised when everyone left quickly and quietly like a crowd breaking up after a funeral service. To make matters worse, I recognized one of the prospective buyers. His father worked days at the plastics factory.

While we were trying to sell our house, Patty's parents were expanding their real estate holdings. Together with a half dozen other couples, they purchased a medium-size seasonal park in the Thousand Islands region of New York. Their "resort" included eight cottages, a dilapidated restaurant, and a trailer park with about twenty house trailers. When the deal closed, the new owners drew straws to see who would get each cottage. Carlin and Sandy ended up with one of the three cottages closest to the water.

Sandy invited us to spend Labor Day weekend with them at the river, figuring we could use a break. The three of us, and Sheba, squeezed into my small pickup truck and headed for the river. As nervous as I was about traveling to a strange place, I kept my mind occupied with the prospect of doing a little fishing, something I'd loved doing with my father as a child. Perhaps Carlin and I could create some fishing memories of our own. The three-hour trip gave Patty and me a chance to talk about the future.

"Do you think the house will sell?" Patty asked.

"It has to," I replied.

"You hear all those stories about houses taking forever to sell . . ."

"I know we're biased, but our little cape has charm. Somebody will see that."

"It'll sell," Patty said wishfully under her breath. "I talked to a friend at work about Sheba. She has a son about ten years old. He'd love to have a dog."

Several miles passed in silence. There it was. Up until this point I refused to allow my mind to entertain such thoughts. How could I ever send her away? I believed we would always be together. A future without Sheba seemed otherworldly.

"Bill, are you okay?"

"I wasn't planning on giving up Sheba. We need to find an apartment that allows dogs."

We drove on. Sheba lay quietly on the floor at Patty's feet not knowing her future with us might be hanging by a thread. Dan slept between me and Patty in his car seat. We turned off the New York State Thruway and headed north on Interstate 81.

The traffic thinned the farther we got from Syracuse. Some of the exits off Interstate 81 directed motorists to the Adirondack Mountains. We weren't close enough to see the mountains, but I did notice some of the leaves had already started changing colors. The prospect of fall seemed to help me relax. We continued to talk as I drove. Topics ranged from what we hoped to do with our jobs, her parents' new property, and what life might be like after we sold the house.

We'd been to Niagara Falls on our honeymoon and watched the water spill over the falls, knowing that it eventually made its way into Lake Ontario. The Thousand Islands region was at the opposite end of the lake where the water flowed down the St. Lawrence River and eventually emptied into the Atlantic Ocean. I was about to discover that the nostalgia of this region rivaled that of Niagara Falls. It was an adventurer's paradise. When we finally set foot on the property, it was like taking a step back in time. The buildings might have thrived in the '60s and '70s, but they had aged rapidly since then.

According to Sandy, the building closest to the road was once a well-known restaurant. Sadly, the dilapidated structure was too far gone to be restored. I held Dan while Patty and her mom picked through the contents of the building for a souvenir. Patty selected a '60s-era percolator along with a handful of other mementos.

Carlin and Sandy's cottage was small, but the space around it would allow room for expansion. Carlin was already making plans to put on an addition. The interior walls were lined with vertical tongue-and-groove pine boards. Aging varnish gave the wood a rich orange-and-yellow finish. The back of the cottage was divided into two small bedrooms, each one just big enough to house a double bed, nightstand, and dresser.

The front of the cottage featured a combined kitchen and living room space. A chrome-and-vinyl dinette set, a sofa, and small '60s-era appliances ate up most of the space. The windows on the north wall of the cottage offered a spectacular view of the river. The view included two large boat docks jetting out into a large bay and several of the islands. Lake freighters made their way through the shipping lanes, passing close enough to spot crew members using binoculars.

The previous owners had added a bathroom in a small corner of the living area. It was one of the smallest bathrooms I'd ever been in. There was just enough space for a sink, a toilet, and a metal box they called a shower. This cottage had charm, and Patty and I loved it.

Later in the day while Dan was napping, I took Sheba down to the river to see how she'd react to the water. I really wanted to see her swim. I produced her favorite toy, a Frisbee, hoping to lure her into the water with it. My first toss landed a few feet in front of her. Without hesitation Sheba plunged into the water and retrieved it. The water came up only to her belly, but it showed me she wasn't afraid of it.

I tossed the Frisbee again. This time about thirty feet away. I was happy to see that it floated. Sheba plunged in after it as I watched it bob on the wavy surface. Once the water reached her neck, she began to swim. Her strokes were smooth and efficient, not much different than if she were walking on land. I was amazed at how effortless she motored over to the Frisbee using four webbed paws.

I had to see more, so I prepared to give her the ultimate test. I walked partway down the main dock and veered onto one of the floating dock fingers free of boats. Sheba followed, wondering what I was up to. I flung the Frisbee about a hundred feet out into the bay. As soon as I let it go, I wondered if I'd made a mistake. Would Sheba even be able to find it, let alone bring it back?

Sheba never hesitated. She leaped off the dock, belly flopped in the water, and swam in a straight line toward the Frisbee. Thankfully, gentle waves presented no challenge. On her way back, the Frisbee acted like a scoop channeling water into her mouth. She quickly adapted by breathing through her nose. It was obvious to me she was a natural born swimmer. I had to remind myself that she'd never been in the water before.

After supper we sat around the table playing cards. The two losers had to do the dishes. I was one of them. Fortunately, I could take in the view of a golden sunset as I dried the dishes. A gentle breeze scuffed the water like coarse sandpaper, allowing the sun's rays to create sparkles on the roughed-up surface. That day I learned how much Patty loved the sparkles on the water.

The next day I asked Carlin to take me to the bait shop in town to get a fishing license. All the talk about how good the fishing was had made me curious. When we returned, Carlin led me down to his boat slip where a fourteen-foot tri-hull, equipped with a thirty-five-horse-power outboard motor, waited for us to climb aboard. The thing had to be as old as I was. The green fiberglass body was faded so badly it was almost the same color as the white hull. He had me sit on a ragged vinyl bench next to the driver's seat that looked like it would collapse any moment. Carlin fiddled with the starter and the choke several times trying to bring the engine to life. Finally, the engine coughed and sputtered before reaching something resembling an idle.

"Are you sure this thing is seaworthy?" I asked.

"She'll float," Carlin said, laughing. "This bay has some of the best fishing."

"That's what I keep hearing. What do people catch here? The water looks shallow."

"About a hundred yards off the shore there's a drop-off. Boats come from all over to fish on that ledge. We catch northern pike and perch in the bay, bass in the weed beds along the shoreline, and out in the main channel there's salmon and muskie."

A taunt anchor held us against the river's current, causing the boat to rock gently. Time felt different while we fished, measured by the pace of the sun and not by the hands of my watch. I was only three hours away from home yet worlds away from my troubles.

In this serene setting God painted a beautiful sunset over our heads, turning the clouds orange, purple, and red. The sound of waves lapping against the side of the boat was peaceful. At no time did I feel judged by Carlin to be a less than capable man because Patty and I were selling our house. Instead, I felt privileged to know him and be married to his daughter. We kept a half dozen of the biggest perch we caught for supper and released the rest of the fish back into the river.

Our weekend getaway was over as quickly as it began. Back home, we resumed our daily grind balancing work and keeping the house clean to show to prospective buyers. Patty and I were getting nervous because we still hadn't received any offers. At the advice of our realtor, Lenny, we scheduled an open house. He said it would drum up new interest in our property.

The day of the open house Patty and I took Sheba and Dan to my parents' house, leaving Lenny alone to schmooze potential buyers. We got a call from Lenny after the open house, telling us we could have our house back. He told us it was well attended and worth the effort. One young couple acted interested and left their contact information but didn't include a realtor. I wondered to myself, *How serious could they be if they were looking for a house without a realtor?*

The next day Lenny followed up with the young couple. Apparently, they wanted to put in an offer on our house but didn't know the proper procedure. Lenny stepped in and helped them write up an offer. We received the offer later that day and tried to keep our excitement in check while we reviewed it. It was a low offer. As I examined the paperwork, I noticed Lenny was now representing both the seller *and* the buyer. We tried to negotiate the price upward, but it was like trying to carry a piano up a staircase. We didn't get very far.

It became apparent to us that the buyers were benefitting more from Lenny's services than we were. He knew how desperate we were to sell, which gave us a weak bargaining position. We debated whether or not to drop Lenny as our realtor, but we were worried the buyers might walk away from the table. In the end, we sold the house to them for considerably less than what we'd hoped. Lenny received a commission from both parties. The whole transaction left a sour taste in my mouth.

If God was involved in all aspects of our lives, why would He let something like this happen? Was he showing me what happens when idols are torn from our grasp? That would account for the sour taste in my mouth and the helplessness I experienced through the whole ordeal. It also occurred to me I might be too focused on the present. Lately, God seemed to be showing me how much of life Patty and I had yet to live. What did God see in our future that we didn't?

As expected, the buyers wanted to move in as soon as possible, which forced us to launch our "move" protocol: find an apartment, stow our possessions, and address Sheba's future. I was disappointed when the only apartment we could find on short notice didn't allow dogs. When the realization hit me that I had to part with Sheba, I was devastated.

Patty reconnected with her friend at work. Melanie, her husband, and their son were eager to take Sheba into their home. When the day came to drop Sheba off at their house, I couldn't bring myself to go with Patty. I was sick to my stomach with grief. To be honest I felt like a pirate forcing his ever-loyal first mate to walk a gang plank to their doom. What kind of person does that to their best friend?

I knelt in front of Sheba and looked into her eyes and told her how much I loved her. I thought about all she'd taught me about love and devotion, which brought tears to my eyes. We'd come so far together. I wrapped my arms around her neck and held her as tears continued to stream down my cheeks. I was mad at myself for having to put her through this. She deserved better. Sheba whined softly yet remained a stoic figure of strength as I melted down in front of her. The pain I felt ran heart-and-soul deep. How could I ever forget her?

Patty bravely transported Sheba to her friend's house. Sheba seemed to know what was happening even before Melanie's son took the leash from Patty. Why else would she yank herself free from the child's grasp and jump back in the car through the partially rolled-up passenger window as Patty backed out of their driveway?

I shed an ocean of tears waiting for Patty to return and was overwhelmed with a sense of loss and regret. Sheba had brought so much joy into my life. I recalled the moment she first looked at me while huddled in a wooden crate with her littermates . . . the smell of her puppy fur . . . her squirms and whimpers when I held her . . . the fun we had chasing softballs . . . catching Frisbees in return for sloppy kisses. I already missed not having her beside me and shadowing my every move. Sheba, as much as Patty, helped me transition from being a young man bound by a marriage covenant to a woman, to being a good friend, husband, and father. I wondered to myself how much more I could have learned from her. What had I done?

~

The buyers moved in right after Thanksgiving. It was emotionally hard vacating our home. The earliest years of our marriage were wrapped up in that house. Now the only thing we had to show for it was a handful of pages in a photo album. As it turned out, the greatest effort wasn't in building our house but in letting go of it. We had learned a brutal lesson about finances.

The euphoria we'd experienced as homeowners made it difficult to adjust to apartment living. We were quickly introduced to the vocal and musical clamor of our fellow renters. It felt odd living in the same building with people we didn't know, whose habits and schedules differed significantly from ours. Their noisy intrusions served as a reminder of what we'd given up.

I deemed our one-year experiment in public housing a flop and equated it with purgatory, suffering for mistakes I'd made. Even in this gray period, however, when neither darkness nor light graced our living arrangement, our financial burden began to lift.

I had a lot of time to think about Sheba and why I didn't try harder to find a way to keep her. I beat myself up badly. One day it occurred to me how fortunate Patty and I were to have a coworker ready and willing to adopt Sheba. Then I considered the boy whose childhood would be greatly impacted by Sheba's company. I also had to consider the possibility that God knew what He was doing. It reminded me of a saying I'd heard: "God is good all the time, all the time God is good."

The travail of letting go of our house and Sheba quickly faded when the news of Patty's second pregnancy flooded our lives like a bright light. It brought peace to our unsettledness. But God blessings didn't end there. Two months before renewing our lease, we were once again made aware of God's perfect timing. Roger, my softball teammate, and his wife were preparing to move out of the house they were renting. He asked us if we were interested in renting it. When I learned the name of the elderly landlord, you could say God winked at me. We'd rented our very first apartment from the same lady five years earlier.

Trust in the LORD with all your heart and lean not on your own understanding. (Proverbs 3:5)

You will surely forget your trouble, recalling it only as waters gone by. Life will be brighter than noonday, and darkness will become like morning. (Job 11:16–17)

"For I know the plans I have for you," declares the LORD, "plans to prosper you and not to harm you, plans to give you hope and a future. Then you will call upon me and come and pray to me, and I will listen to you." (Jeremiah 29:11–12)

FIVE

A Sheepherder

THE OLD HOUSE we rented had to have been at least a hundred years old. It was originally one of a handful of houses dotting Main Street back at the turn of the twentieth century. Someone built a wall down the middle of this once grand dwelling decades ago and converted it into a duplex. This would account for the odd layout of rooms measuring half their former size. Its old-world charm reminded me of my grandparents' house: fuzzy antique wallpaper, elaborate wall moldings, creaky floorboards, large drafty windows, and a quirky staircase that made a dangerous ninety-degree turn about a third of the way up. For the time being this was our place, and it felt like home.

I wasn't looking forward to wasting years of my life trying to accumulate enough money to make a down payment on another house. Selling our first house was a setback any way I looked at it, but I only needed to look into the eyes of my boys to know that I'd do it all over again for them. In practically no time at all we made great strides toward the endeavor of purchasing another home partly due to our successes at work. It also helped that our rent was very low. Patty found the part-time work she wanted, and I had all the overtime I could handle at the plastics factory.

In the four years since we sold our house, so much of our lives had changed. The birth of Mike was without a doubt the most significant event. Time moved quickly as we tried to keep pace with our two young boys. We were making memories every day without realizing it.

Patty and I loved the old house we rented. It had a small side yard where Dan and Mike played in a sandbox, swam in a plastic pool, and swung in a tire suspended from a tree limb. I enjoyed the afternoons I spent with the boys giving them motorcycle rides around the yard, wrestling with them on the floor, and to a lesser degree watching *Sesame Street* and *Mr. Rogers* on television. Surrounded by crumbling stone walls in the basement, I started a small model train layout with Dan.

We wanted the best for our children, which for us equated to buying another house for them to grow up in. So, we started looking at small houses, ones that wouldn't require a significant increase in Patty's work hours. We finally found one the realtor deemed a "starter" home. A tiny house on a tiny lot with no garage in an old suburban neighborhood. The only real feature it had going for it was the asking price. Our offer was accepted.

After waiting for almost two months for our mortgage lender's approval, we learned there was a problem with the financing. It had nothing to do with us. As a result, our purchase offer expired before we received a mortgage commitment letter. The day our offer expired, the owner of the property withdrew her house from the market. Apparently, she no longer wished to sell it. Because the events that transpired were so strange, Patty and I wondered if God might be leading us in another direction. As it turned out, God did have something special in mind for us.

"Can you believe we are about to own another brand-new house again?" I asked.

"It does seem like a dream," Patty replied. "But I am going to miss this place."

"I never thought I'd say this, but we've made a lot of memories here," I added.

Lorraine, a realtor Patty stumbled on in our housing search, represented a home builder who was constructing a new housing development, which oddly enough was about a mile from our first house. This was the same builder who'd built a house for my parents in 1962 when I was a boy. The "coincidences" were piling up.

Of all the places we could buy a dwelling, why was this house so close to our first place? Was God making sure we connected the two residences—one sacrificed for the good of our family and one intended to serve as the restoration of former things? And what about the builder who connected my past with our future? When I realized God had not left us to fend for ourselves, the thought overwhelmed me.

Patty leaned back in the swing on the porch of our old rental and set it in motion. The chains dangling from hooks anchored to the ceiling groaned as we swung back and forth. I put my arm around her and pumped my legs just enough to keep the swing moving. A refreshing breeze brushed against my face. Dan and Mike played on the other side of the screen door, building something out of a pile of toy blocks. It was a memorable moment in time, a peaceful evening, one of the few nights Patty and I got to spend together without one of us having to get ready for work.

I tried to take in every detail of the world around me as the evening shadows crept over the lawn. A lone cricket chirped in a nearby flower bed beckoning for the darkness to come. Patty pointed at a butterfly combing the surface of a flower whose petals were about to close.

"Don't you find it ironic we couldn't get a bank to move fast enough on the used house we tried to buy, but we could get financing on a new one even before the house was built?" I said.

"I'm sure that wasn't a coincidence," Patty countered.

"Explain to me again how we qualified for a first-time home-owner mortgage."

"It was in the fine print. Because we hadn't owned a home for three years, they considered us first-time homebuyers. We are one of two families granted special financing in the whole housing development."

As it turned out, the past four years weren't wasted at all; they had a specific purpose. Who but God could number our years and determine each year's significance? I wondered why He took such an interest in my life, and I found myself questioning how much I really knew of His ways.

Patty nestled her head against my chest. Her damp hair carried the scent of her shampoo. I noticed she was spinning the rings on her finger. She often did this when she was thinking about us or our future.

I thought about our first house and the plot of land on which it stood. It felt like a distant memory now, something we'd done in a previous life. I found it quite revealing that I missed Sheba more than the house. I vowed to myself that if we ever got another dog, we'd have a safety net to fall back on. I wouldn't be able to live with myself if I had to rehome another dog.

The following week, after all the legal papers were signed, we moved into a brand-new house. We felt like VIPs setting foot in a palace. This time someone else had built a house for us. It was hard not to make comparisons to our first house. Both were Cape Cods featuring a set of stairs just inside the front door leading to a second floor. The floor plans were almost identical: a kitchen and living room on one end, a bathroom in the middle, and two bedrooms at the end of a short hallway. Could this be why we felt so at home from the very first day? This house wasn't just as good as our first one; it was better because it came with an attached two-car garage.

August was typically the hottest month in Western New York, and rainfall was sparse. If people watered their lawns in August, it was to keep their grass alive. They wouldn't think about starting a new lawn unless they had to. We had to. Our residence came with a freshly seeded lawn, which amounted to dirt painted green from the mixture of fertilizer and grass seed. I was told by the builder to keep the dirt wet for two to three weeks. Patty and I, not the builder, would be paying the county's water authority for every drop of water we used.

As a boy I learned the song "Row, Row, Row Your Boat." It was popular to sing the song in a round. One person started the song, and a second person joined in after a few bars. For Patty and me the lyrics amounted to "move, move, move the sprinklers as water flowed gently from the tap." We found out it was nearly impossible to keep grass seed moist while the sun baked the soil.

While we waited for the grass to grow, the boys would play either in the garage, in the basement, or in their sandbox in the back-yard. Patty and I would continually move the sprinklers until we covered the entire yard with water, and then we would start the process over again.

No sooner had we settled into our daily routine as new home-owners when my work schedule changed. I was asked by the vice president of our company to switch shifts again, this time to work evenings from three p.m. to eleven p.m. I was finally going to be given a chance to prove myself as a supervisor. Our plastics factory ventured into a new type of work: labeling and repackaging products for other companies. I knew I was ready for the challenge and agreed to do it without hesitation. I had to supervise a dozen brand-new workers, and I was given a significant pay raise. It was my job to shape them into productive workers. My body thanked me immedi-ately for not being forced to stay awake all hours of the night, while my heart thanked God for another blessing.

On weekends when our family was all together, we watched nature shows on public television. We loved the series they showed on work dogs. One episode featured Border Collies and their role as sheepherders. The program portrayed these dogs as loyal creatures with an intense desire to please their owners. Patty and I thought it might be time to get another dog. We both had dogs as children and wanted our boys to have the same experience. *A Border Collie might be a good fit for the kids*, we figured, and we joked that a dog with herding skills might help us keep track of them.

By Labor Day the grass was sprouting, giving our lawn the

appearance of a bald man attempting to grow hair. Patty wanted to take Dan and Mike to see her parents over the holiday weekend. I stayed behind to maintain my vigil of wetting the dirt. Before she left, I happened to notice an ad in the local Penny Saver. Someone was selling Border Collie pups. From the price they were asking, I assumed they weren't purebreds, but that wouldn't matter to two young boys.

With Patty's blessing, I planned to go see the puppies while the kids were away. I thought it might be good to know what we were getting into before two young hearts were broken. My trek that Saturday took me deep into Upstate New York farm country. My eyes soaked up the scenery as I drove. My drive was a welcome break from my vigil of moving hoses around the yard.

High above me the sun played hide-and-seek behind the puffy white clouds moving in packs across a bright blue sky. The landscape offered an ever-changing panorama of woods, crop fields, and fenced pastures. The road itself seemed to be woven into the fabric of the landscape, rising, falling, twisting, and turning with the terrain.

Eventually, I reached my destination by following vague hand-written directions scribbled on a piece of paper. A farmer rocking on a porch swing stood up and made his way onto the gravel driveway with a dog at his side. He was an older gentleman, probably in his sixties, wearing a baseball cap with a frayed bill, a well-worn T-shirt, coveralls, and boots caked with mud. He extended a friendly hand and offered me a smile.

We talked briefly about the weather and where I hailed from before the conversation made its way to the puppies. He gestured toward a pasture while we talked. A horse was moving erratically just outside a barn. When I looked closer, I could see the source of its distress. A brown-and-white Border Collie was barking at its heels intensely practicing its craft. It was the mother of the puppies I'd come to see.

"That dog will try to herd anything," he said, chuckling.

"Do you still have puppies for sale?" I asked.

"Isn't that what you came for?" he said, moving toward the barn. "Follow me."

Caught up in the moment, I counted out fifty dollars and placed the money in the farmer's hand. Moments later I walked back to my decade-old pickup carrying a black-and-white puppy in my arms. Later that evening I telephoned Patty with the news.

"I went to see the puppies today."

"What did you think of them?"

"I got carried away and bought one."

"Hey, I thought you were going to wait until I saw them!"

"It turned out to be an hour drive each way. I wasn't sure when we'd be able to get back there again. You're not mad me, are you?"

"No. I'm just a little disappointed, that's all."

"Dan and Mike will go crazy when they see her."

"Where's the puppy now?" Patty asked.

"I'm building a pen for her in the garage."

"Good. Don't forget she's been raised outside on a farm, and we don't need any surprises."

When Dan and Mike returned home, their eyes grew wide with excitement having spotted a puppy living in their garage. They hugged and tugged on the furry bundle. It was probably the first time our new puppy had been exposed to that much attention. Her tail never stopped wagging.

At the dinner table that evening a naming convention broke out. Patty and I knew it would be one of those priceless moments because the boys were so young.

"What do you think we should call our new puppy?" Patty asked.

I jumped into the conversation and said, "I think we should call her Blacky."

"No, Daddy, we need to name her Lady!" Dan countered adamantly.

"Why would we call her that?" I replied.

"Because she's Lady," he answered.

"That's not a reason. What about Spot or Patches?" I said. "Those are good names."

"Daddy, she's Yady," two-year-old Mike said, chiming in.

"Bill, I think they've already decided," Patty said, trying to put an end to my teasing.

"Are you sure you want to call her Lady? We can't call her Lady today and something else tomorrow."

"Daddy, she's Lady," Dan insisted, on the verge of tears.

Patty and I were not surprised they were so resolute about the name. The animated Disney film *Lady and the Tramp* was a family favorite. Lady, one of the story's main characters, was the most heroic dog they knew in their short lives. I hoped our sons would experience in real life the love they saw acted out on the movie screen. And if "Lady" acted anything like the dog in the movie, she would steal their hearts and be the recipient of a double blessing.

About a week after Lady came into our lives, I noticed tiny bite marks on the boy's arms and legs. It wasn't until I felt something crawling up my leg that I remembered Patty's words: "Keep the puppy out of the house; we don't want any surprises." Sure enough, we had a flea outbreak. I took the boys to my parents', but not before setting off flea bombs in every room of the house. After that episode, we were vigilant about Lady's flea prevention treatments. I discovered that it took much longer mentally to be rid of the idea of fleas in the house than it did to eradicate them. Every itch or inkling of something crawling on your person required a full investigation to regain our peace of mind.

For the next several weeks I stood on the sidelines and watched the bond deepen between Lady and our children. I remembered the similar experience I'd had with Sheba. I did not have to encourage Dan and Mike to play with her. They included her in everything they did.

When the grass was thick enough to play on, one of the boys' favorite activities was coasting down our gently sloping side yard on whatever toy they could ride. Dan, pencil thin and almost ready to start kindergarten, could handle the slope by himself. Mike had to be guided down with my help. Lady took a liking to chasing Dan as he rode down the slope. She nipped at his shorts while he cruised and bowled him over with kisses once he stopped moving. I looked on as Dan rolled around on the ground laughing as he trying to get back up to ride down the hill again.

Mike, a redhead still carrying some of his baby fat, had the prettiest blue eyes I ever saw. He was almost out of diapers, and his idea of fun involved pushing around a large metal Tonka dump truck. If he found something in the yard, he'd give it a ride in the bed of the truck. Lady, ever curious, took a keen interest in whatever Mike was transporting.

Mike's signature belly laugh filled the garage one day as he tried to keep Lady away from the toad he'd found while playing in the dirt. He scooped up "Toady" and put him in the bed of the dump truck. Needless to say, Toady had a very bumpy ride. Mike stopped occasionally to lift the creature out of the bed of the truck and examine it to see if it was okay. With his limited vocabulary, he lectured Lady to stay away from Toady. He held the toad in an open hand as he showed it to the puppy. The toad, sensing his freedom was one leap away, jumped. Mike tackled Lady to keep her from getting the toad. During the melee, the toad somehow managed to a make a clean getaway. While a pool of tears was being shed, I intervened and offered my condolences.

Patty and I routinely used Lady as an example of how to be a responsible pet owner. We taught our children to be sure Lady always had water in her bowl and reminded them that Mommy and Daddy had to feed her every day. I always got a kick out of watching them pretend to take care of her. They'd speak to Lady as if she were a person while they pretended to feed her.

Mike still had a limited understanding of how to care for Lady and what rules needed to be strictly adhered to. Mimicking Mommy and Daddy was his way of learning. Lady was learning life lessons as well. One of the things she learned was to stand by the door when she needed to go to the bathroom. Mike was too young to understand that you just couldn't let the dog outside. In our case, this was an open invitation for our puppy to run off. Lady, when offered her freedom, lit out of the house like a horse bolting from a barn.

The town we lived in had a leash law, which required dog owners to leash their pets when not on their property. It would be well within their right for a neighbor to call the dog warden if they saw a dog loose in their yard. Fortunately for us, when Lady got loose, Patty or I would provide our neighbors with some entertainment chasing our dog around the neighborhood. We were often barefoot and under-dressed. The pain of chasing Lady over gravel driveways and through prickly hedgerows in bare feet is not something you easily forgot. It took several "escapes" before I finally got the point across to Mike.

Even when a situation was under control, accidents still happened. Lady snuck out through a partially open kitchen door while Dan was practicing his bike riding skills in the garage. Lady bolted into our neighbor's yard, and Dan dropped his bike and gave chase. Our neighbor, whom we called Miss D, had a pair of Great Danes. Her dogs were able to roam freely in her yard because she had invisible fencing. Unfortunately, invisible fencing did nothing to prevent Lady from entering their yard.

Dan stood on the property line calling out to Lady and pleading for her to come back. When the Great Danes saw our dog, they charged after her. Lady was still playfully young and enjoyed barking at other dogs. Curious, the Great Danes came over to investigate.

When I heard yelling, crying, barking, and yelping drifting in through our bedroom window, I ran outside to investigate. I was unsure what I could do against two large dogs. They could reach my throat without leaping. I ventured into my neighbor's yard tentatively without anything to defend myself. Thankfully, Miss D heard the commotion at the same time I did and came to my rescue. The dogs were quickly separated, and I was relieved that Lady was not seri-ously injured. Dan watched the whole incident, standing on the prop-erty line and melting in a pool of tears. He felt responsible. I apologized profusely to Miss D for Lady wandering into her yard. She bore us no ill will because she loved our boys.

Feeling bad for Dan, I vowed to finally do something about

Lady's tendency to escape. A dog or a child could be seriously hurt the next time this happened. I determined that the best option was to purchase an outdoor dog kennel and attach it to the garage. To gain access to the kennel, I cut a small opening in the garage wall for Lady to let herself out into the kennel. I also constructed a smaller pen inside the garage so that Lady could be safely contained if the kids were playing with the garage door open.

To keep the bad weather out, I installed a clear vinyl flap, which the kids affectionately called the "doggy door." Lady, however, was afraid of the plastic flap. I credit the boys for climbing in the kennel and helping Lady overcome her fear.

≈

When I brought Lady home from the farm, our children felt as much at home in Lady's pen as they did in their own bedrooms. Our puppy and the boys were inseparable. She taught them how to love and be loved. Lady followed the boys wherever they went and would eventually sleep in Dan's bed.

I gained valuable insight watching our boys interact with their dog. I could see things, simple things, that made my children's relationship with their dog stronger. Because they were young and their lives were much less complicated than mine, Dan and Mike were able to devote more time to Lady than I ever could to Sheba. The boys conversed with their dog like she was a person, played with her, and involved her in everything they did. Our sheepherder's interaction with Dan and Mike modeled the love and companionship of the Good Shepherd spoken of in the Bible (John 10:11-14).

As I took all this in, I examined my relationship with God. Even though I felt I was traveling on the path God had laid out for me, I wanted to draw closer to Him, to involve God in more of my life. As a result, I got more involved at our church. I volunteered in the nursery with Patty, mowed the church lawn, served on the board of trustees, and taught an occasional adult Sunday school class. I wasn't trying to earn God's favor; I just wanted him to know how grateful I was and to show my children the importance of being involved in something you believed in.

I can remember watching my father serve at our church when I was a boy. Like Dad, I became interested in studying my Bible and searching for a deeper understanding of its meaning. I wanted to be able to apply Scripture to events I encountered in my life.

This was the life I dreamed about as a child. This is the life I was living.

The LORD is my shepherd, I lack nothing. He makes me lie down in green pastures, he leads me beside quiet waters, he refreshes my soul. He guides me along the right paths for his name's sake. (Psalm 23:1–3)

Be shepherds of God's flock that is under your care, watching over them—not because you must, but because you are willing, as God wants you to be; not pursuing dishonest gain, but eager to serve. (1 Peter 5:2)

As a father has compassion on his children, so the LORD has compassion on those who fear him. (Psalm 103:13)

SIX

This Little Light of Mine

A WET NOSE touched my arm arousing me from sleep. If Lady, now two years old was whining and carrying on, it meant either she wanted to go outside or something was wrong. I looked at my watch. It was midnight. I tried to recall if anyone had let her out before we all went to bed. I guess it didn't matter.

I rolled out of the water bed and thought the air in the room was cooler than usual. Maybe it was just my imagination. I didn't want to wake up Patty, so I felt around on the floor for my slippers and ventured out into the hallway without turning on any lights. A loud crack startled me. *Was that gunfire? Fireworks? Who would be setting off fireworks on a Sunday evening in March at midnight?* I was confused.

I flicked on the light switch in the kitchen, but nothing happened. *Something must have tripped the circuit breaker.* I tried the lights in the living room. Nothing. *The power must be out.*

That wasn't good. Tonight, of all nights, I needed my alarm clock to be working. I had to be on time for work in the morning. Jim, my boss, was counting on me being there. Another crack broke the silence. *What was going on?*

Sales from our company's packaging division were about to

surpass those of the injection molding division. The packaging business had expanded so rapidly that we had to move all the equipment and inventory into its own building across town.

To further complicate matters, we won a bid to assemble disposable camera chassis for a well-known film company. Photo developers were already processing these cameras by removing the roll of film and discarding the plastic camera carcasses. Pop culture rushed to embrace the disposable camera market. It was exciting to know we'd be part of something trending in magazine ads. I was told growth of the disposable cameras was projected to be in the millions of units each year. Later this morning we were scheduled to build our first batch of camera chassis under the supervision of the film company.

I still worked the afternoon shift, but my boss wanted me to be on hand in the event any bigwigs from the film company attended the proceedings. We wanted to make a big impression and demonstrate we had the capability to assemble the cameras on our second shift if needed.

Another loud crack startled me. *What in the world is happening?* I needed to find out what was going on outside. I grabbed a flashlight out of my sock drawer and headed back to the kitchen. Lady nervously followed my every step. I heard two more cracks. *That's not gunfire.* I lifted the telephone off the receiver. *That's odd, the telephone is dead too.* I paused to listen to the rain striking the roof. It made an unusual ticking sound. *Is that sleet?*

I stuck my head out the front door but couldn't see a thing. The world outside was completely black; even the expressway lights off in the distance were out. My flashlight beam caught one of our young maple trees in the front yard. The twenty-foot arbor bowed under the weight of the ice, coating its branches, and was bent in the shape of a *U.* I waved the flashlight around searching for the other two trees. They were in the same condition. Another loud crack echoed through the house. Suddenly, it all made sense. Freezing rain was bringing down the trees. The weight of the accumulating ice was also bringing down the power lines.

Lady stood behind me and continued to whine. *I might as well let her out while I'm up.* She followed me out into the garage. Since no one else was up this time of night, I opened the back door to let her roam free. When Lady dropped down to one first step, her feet skated out from underneath her. She slid down the remaining stair treads, landing in a heap on the ice-covered grass. With great difficulty Lady struggled to her feet.

"It's okay, girl. Go potty."

Lady sniffed and moved awkwardly like someone wearing roller skates for the first time. When she finished her business, she tried to ascend the first of three steps but was unsuccessful. She began to whine as the freezing rain continued to pelt her.

I grabbed the ice-covered handrail and attempted to lower myself down one step. There were no treads on my slippers. Even if there were, I'm not sure it would have made any difference. Once I transferred my weight onto the stair tread, my foot slipped off, I lost my balance, and my butt landed in the gap between the first and second treads of the stairs.

"Ouch! This stuff is nasty."

The freezing rain was now pelting me as I pulled myself to a sitting position on the second tread. Lady stood at the base of the stairs unsure of what to do. I wasn't sure either. Instinctively, I gripped the rail with one hand and extended my free hand toward Lady, attempting to grab her by the collar. I'd seen rescue attempts like this in the movies.

"Come here, girl, it's all right."

Reluctantly, Lady put her front feet on the bottom step and drew within reach. I began to shiver as the rain had soaked through what little clothing I had on. My pajama bottoms felt like they were stuck to the icy stair.

"Forgive me, Lady, but I have to do this."

I grabbed Lady by the collar and drew her up into my lap. Then I leaned back against the steps and heaved her up over my shoulders in the direction of the door opening. She caromed off the partially open door and landed in a heap on the concrete floor. Lady shook out her coat and wagged her tail. She seemed to appreciate being able to stand on solid ground again.

It was my turn to move. With both hands I grabbed the handrail, gripping it like a vise, and pulled myself to a standing position. I slowly pivoted like a ballerina and faced the door opening. Leaning forward, I transferred my grip to the door casing, first with one hand and then the other. It was pointless to rely on my feet for assistance, so I pulled myself through the doorway using all the strength I had in my arms.

"Are you all right, girl?"

I toweled both of us off and changed into a dry pair of sweats. The temperature inside was getting cooler because our gas furnace needed electricity to function. But that wasn't my main concern. I needed to make it to work in the morning on time, so I set off in search of a windup alarm clock that I knew was somewhere in our bedroom.

The events of the past hour had certainly shortened the life of the battery in the flashlight. I decided to catch a few winks in the living room and preserve the flashlight battery. It would be good to know when the electricity was restored, so I turned on some of the lights in the room. When I finally lowered myself into a recliner and pulled an Afghan over me, I prayed, *God, please don't let me oversleep.* Lady stretched out on the floor beside me. The last thing I remembered was reaching down to scratch her head.

I woke up before the sun was up. The alarm hadn't gone off yet. It was strange not hearing traffic on the expressway. There wasn't any sound at all anywhere. With nothing else to do, I got up and did a little recon. The electricity and the phone were still out. I ventured into the basement to check the water level in the crock that housed our sump pump. It was almost dry. While I was down there, I looked around our laundry room for the old oil lamp my mother claimed was a family heirloom. It would be worth something today if it worked. I was pleased to find it half full of lamp oil. Placing it on the kitchen table, I went in search of a box of matches.

I wondered how much of the area was without power and if there was any way to find out how long we might be without it. As I sat at the kitchen table fiddling with the oil lamp, I wondered what my next move should be. Perhaps a shower would help me focus. I might as well get dressed for work while I was at it. Anticipating an icy cold experience, I was pleasantly surprised to learn that our gas hot water heater was still functioning. My mind raced as the hot water ran over my head.

The best way to get the news if we didn't have access to the television, was the radio. It seemed like the best radio option without waking up the house might be the car. It turned out to be an apocalyptic experience sitting in the front seat of our Dodge K-car channel surfing for a radio station in the middle of a blackout. When I found one, I listened for about ten minutes.

The damage was incredible. They were dubbing it the storm of the century, a once-in-a-hundred-year ice storm. All the counties in western New York State were affected. Telephone poles had snapped, live wires lay arcing on the ground, and trees were down, making many of the roads impassable. One announcer said it could be days or weeks before the electricity was restored. It didn't seem possible what they were saying was true, but I had to concede that our power and telephone were out.

I wanted to contact my boss, but I knew it would be an exercise in futility. If it weren't for the state of emergency in effect, I could try driving to work. I wasn't going anywhere.

It was too cold to continue listening to the car radio and I didn't want to run down the battery, so I went inside and dug through our closet to a portable AM radio. The radio announcers on WHAM 1180 AM read cancellations nonstop for forty-five minutes, pausing only to give updates on the storm's devastation before resuming their list. There were so many cancellations, the radio personalities had to take turns because they were getting hoarse. A sense of relief washed over me when I heard my company was closed. Every school was closed as well.

I woke up Dan and Mike to share the good news with them. I could see the euphoria building as they became fully awake.

"Daddy, can we watch cartoons?" Dan asked.

"There's no electricity," I replied.

"I'm hungry," Mike added, rubbing his eyes.

"Let's go see if we can find something to eat," I said.

I was thankful Patty hadn't had to work last night and face the possibility of being stranded at the hospital. I knew she'd appreciate being able to sleep in, so I closed the bedroom door. Dan and Mike were gazing into the refrigerator with the door standing wide open when I caught up with them in the kitchen. Without power, we'd have to limit our use of the refrigerator. I reached in and grabbed a milk jug and told them to keep the door closed. I set three bowls and a box of Honey Nut Cheerios on the table.

"Is this stuff any good?" I asked.

"Yeah, Mom buys it for us all the time," Dan replied.

I caught a glimpse of the coffeemaker and stared at it longingly.

"Well, the electricity may be out for a couple of days."

"Cool! Does that mean we won't have school?"

"It sure looks like it. So, we're going to need to follow a couple of special rules until the power comes back on. Rule number one, don't touch the oil lamp on the table. You'll get burned. Mike, are you listening?"

"Yes, Daddy."

"Rule number two, don't open the refrigerator door unless we tell you to. Got it?"

"Yes, Dad," Dan said.

After breakfast I enlisted the boys' help to grab some of our camping equipment out of the garage. They gave me a bewildered look when I told them we were going to camp out in the living room. As I was sorting through the cabinet, I felt the boys' excitement begin to rub off on me. We were going on an adventure together.

I handed each of them a sleeping bag and told them to go pick out a spot in the living room. To my delight I spotted our liquid-fueled camping lantern and stove. I set them aside and continued rummaging. After digging out two more sleeping bags, I struck gold.

"Halleluiah!" I said, holding up a beat-up aluminum drip coffeemaker. "Now, this is a family heirloom."

The sun poured in through the windows and began to warm the living room. Outside, the temperature had risen to almost forty degrees, but inside the thermostat held steady at sixty-five. Dan and Mike dragged their play tent out of the bedroom and put their sleeping bags inside. Lady got barricaded in the tent with them.

Practically drooling at the prospect of having a cup of coffee, I went straight to work assembling the camp stove. I pressurized the fuel tank and lit the burner with a match. I wasn't about to wait until Patty woke up. Just as I was taking my first sip of insanely strong coffee, Patty stumbled into the living room.

"Bill, there's something wrong with the water bed heater. It's too cold."

"The power is out."

"What's going on here?" she said, looking at the mess we'd created in the living room.

"We're camping!" Dan replied, poking his head out of the tent.

"Don't you think this is going a little overboard? And why aren't you getting ready for school?"

"Babe, there is no school. They say the power might be out for days," I said.

"What?"

"They are calling it the ice storm of the century. The phone is dead. We've got no heat, but we do have hot water."

I turned off the handheld radio and offered Patty a cup of coffee.

"Boys, rule three, don't turn on this radio without our permission. We don't want to waste the battery," I said.

"What happened to rules one and two?" Patty asked.

"Ask them," I said, pointing to Dan and Mike.

Patty sipped her coffee and checked out the food situation. She thought we'd have enough food for a few days. I took some of the perishables out of the refrigerator and carried them into the garage where they'd stay cool.

I wanted to go outside and see for myself how bad things looked in our neighborhood. Patty suggested we should do it as a family. We dressed the boys in their winter gear and headed outside. Dan held Lady's leash as we walked. The entire landscape was covered with a thick coat of ice, which caused objects to glisten in the bright sunlight. Carefully, I broke up the ice pinning the tops of our maple trees to the ground. One by one they catapulted themselves upright, causing ice to fly off each trunk.

Our housing development appeared unscathed. Our houses were constructed with underground electric, so there were no downed power lines to worry about. Most of our neighbors' trees were young and flexible enough to take the weight of the ice. The only sound we heard was chain saws running off in the distance. To us it looked like a beautiful early spring day. We walked a third of a mile around to the back of the development where a long narrow strip of woods separated our development from the expressway. It was surreal catching a glimpse of the damage caused to the patch of woods.

"So, this is what all the radio chatter was about last night," I said.

Some trees were uprooted, and many were snapped in half. There were downed limbs everywhere.

"I could hear trees snapping in the middle of the night. At first it sounded like gunfire."

Overall, day one was a good one. Our spirits were high. The sun stayed out, giving us plenty of solar gain, which raised the temperature inside to seventy degrees. With food, water, nontraditional lighting, and the radio, Patty and I felt we could survive easily for a couple of days. As evening approached, Dan and Mike succumbed to cabin fever. Cut off from their electronics and television, they were bored. They resorted to building a fort using blankets and sofa cushions. Lady became the fort's first prisoner.

I must admit there was something romantic about crawling into a double sleeping bag with my spouse and snuggling up together. That was, right up to the point when Patty put her icy cold feet on my calves. I vowed to myself that I wouldn't complain.

Day two was overcast, and the inside temperature never climbed back up from its overnight slide. Sixty degrees doesn't sound cold until you're forced to live in it. Radio programs offered survival tips and reminded people that things like cash registers in grocery stores and gas pumps at filling stations needed electricity to function. Some retail establishments were handling cash transactions only.

The number one problem homeowners faced while without power was keeping their basements from flooding because their sump pumps couldn't run. The fire department kept busy helping utility companies clear debris off the roads and pumping out flooded basements. Ironically, the crock in our basement was still almost dry.

By day three the novelty of our camping experience had completely worn off. We woke up to an indoor temperature in the low fifties. I got nervous when I saw that overnight the water level had risen to the top of the crock. I added bailing water from the crock to my routine. Patty and the boys donned their winter gear inside. That night a hot bath temporarily lifted everyone's spirits. Before bed we played a board game by the light of a camping lantern.

The power came on briefly while we were playing Candyland but went out a few seconds later. The flickering lights lifted our spirits. It was a weird sensation, akin to being trapped in a cave with rescuers giving us a signal that help was on the way.

Sometime in the wee hours of morning the power came back on. Bright light flooded our living room. We danced around the living room with joy. Patty and I vowed to never again take little things in life for granted, like fresh-brewed coffee, a perfectly browned slice of toast, a warm bed, or a brightly lit room. Even though our power was restored, it would be several more days before schools and businesses reopened.

Eventually, things got back to normal and the kids returned to school. Mike signed up to take care of the class pet over Easter break. The experience of having a hamster in the house stirred the boys' interest in having hamsters of their own. As parents we were determined to expose our children to as many things as possible. Because we were committed to that philosophy, it occasionally put us in a position of agreeing to something we'd normally say no to.

Our kids didn't have to beg. We went to the pet store and

purchased two teddy bear hamsters for them. Patty and I lectured them on the importance of keeping them fed, watered, and living in a clean cage. They picked out a Habitrail cage, one of those space-age-looking plastic enclosures with plastic tubes a hamster could travel through to visit other chambers.

These cute creatures did not go unnoticed by Lady. She watched with great interest as they scurried from one compartment to another. She trembled with desire whenever one of them ran on the exercise wheel. The addition of hamsters to our family meant that Lady couldn't sleep in the boys' bedroom any longer.

Several weeks later, on a Saturday morning, I woke to the sound of Dan shouting. I heard the words, "Lady! How could you!"

One of the hamsters had chewed off a piece of the cage's latching mechanism during the night and proceeded to make a jail break. Unbeknownst to the little creature, the warden waited on the other side of the boys' bedroom door. Lady pounced on the creature when it tried to make its getaway. She evidently mouthed the creature until it stopped squeaking.

Dan brought the wet, lifeless form to me in his cupped hands wanting to know if it was dead. Lady trotted proudly behind him believing congratulations and perhaps a treat were in order. She had single-handedly captured the critter and saved the household from a rodent infestation.

Dan and Mike learned a lot about pain, loss, and the natural order of things that day. Lady was loved by them too much not to be forgiven.

When spring gave way to summer, we traveled on weekends when our schedules allowed. My parents, Bill, and Wanda, owned a cottage on Lake Ontario. It was a popular choice for us when all we could manage was an overnight stay. The short one-hour trip offered a change of scenery and a taste of cottage living in the country. The boys and I launched model rockets whenever the weather permitted it.

Watching Dan and Mike play with Lady rekindled my memories of Sheba, and I wondered how my old friend was getting along in her new home. Patty no longer worked with Melanie, the gal who'd taken Sheba in, so we hadn't received any updates for quite a while. I decided that on our next trip to my parents' cottage we'd stop by Sheba's home to see if she remembered me. Patty didn't share my enthusiasm and wondered if it was a good idea.

When we entered Melanie's driveway, it seemed like no one was home, but to my surprise Sheba appeared in the yard. I approached my old friend with glee and called out her name. She was still beautiful, but the fur on her muzzle had started to turn white.

Sheba barked when I approached, causing a flood of happy memories. I continued my advance without a care in the world until it became clear she was not welcoming me. She barred her teeth and growled, making it clear I was not to come any closer. I dropped to one knee and stretched my hand, hoping she'd remember my smell. Her tail never wagged. She kept her distance and growled. I supposed I couldn't blame her. I'd never returned to see her after we parted company.

Was I being naive believing we could just pick up our friendship as if nothing ever happened? I stood up and gazed at her with love in my eyes, much as a person stands in a cemetery and lingers in front of the tombstone of a loved one. A tear formed in the corner of my eye when I realized she served a different master now. I walked away feeling like someone had recorded over a video tape of all my precious memories of her. It was the last time I ever saw Sheba.

The years tumbled by—good years, some of the best years of my life. It pleased me to see that Dan and Mike never outgrew their love for Lady even though their interests were constantly changing. She was theirs for life. My one desire during this time was to make sure I spent time with my kids while they still lived at home. If they ever got lost in their life's travels, I hoped they'd be willing and able to find their way back home.

～

Light

After a week's postponement, we built our first batch of one-time-use camera chassis. In fact, we built thousands of units the first year and quickly made camera assembly a two-shift operation. Cleanup from the damage caused by the ice storm continued for months. Utility crews came from all over the eastern United States to assist our utility company. Together they replaced telephone poles and blown transformers and repaired downed electric lines.

A veil of darkness encroached on our happiness not only during the power outage but also when Dan's hamster died, and my visit to Sheba ended in disappointment. How often do we wish for things to return to the way they were when heartbreaking things happen? The world doesn't stop when darkness comes into our life; it continues, with or without us.

When dark times come, we search for a source of light to help us navigate through them. This light source can be artificial and temporary like a flashlight or permanent and real like a relationship.

Lady was a source of light during our dark times. She remained faithfully by our side during the power outage. When Dan's hamster was killed, Lady took the blame but remained at Dan's side and continued loving on him. When I felt rejected by Sheba, Lady was there affirming that I still had her for companionship. She was a faithful light, ever present with us, and wasn't consumed by the bad things happening around her. Her example reminded me of how important it is to stay attuned to God's light. His light consumes the darkness around us and can cause us to shine (2 Corinthians 4:6) so that we can be a light for others. If we abide with God during dark times, He will be an ever-present light to guide us.

It was easy for me to give God credit for the good things that were happening in my life. Goodness is part of God's very nature. It's a tough thing to grasp that even our bad experiences, disappointments, and tragedies can be used by a good God to accomplish something good (Romans 8:28).

I had changed. Some might argue I finally grew up. My old ways were disappearing and God's ways, though hard for me to cope with sometimes, brought me comfort knowing that my life was unfolding according to His plan. I wondered from time to time if that plan would ever include another dog like Sheba.

I saw that wisdom is better than folly, just as light is better than darkness. (Ecclesiastes 2:13)

For God, who said, "Let light shine out of darkness," made his light shine in our hearts to give us the light of knowledge of God's glory displayed in the face of Christ. (2 Corinthians 4:6)

When Jesus spoke again to the people, he said, "I am the light of the world. Whoever follows me will never walk in darkness, but will have the light of life." (John 8:12)

SEVEN

I Chose You

MOST DAYS, I grabbed lunch with my boss, now vice president of our company, at a local diner during the noon hour. Jim's looks, age, and antics, including his cackle for a laugh, reminded me so much of my grandfather. If I was with Jim, I didn't need to worry about rushing through lunch unless I had a meeting scheduled. He was trying to teach me to pace myself and to leave work at the office. I guess he saw the pressure I was under and didn't want to see me burn out. He led by example, so it was not surprising that today he was on vacation. Put off by the notion of eating alone, I decided to join a handful of the corporate office staff already eating in the company break room.

Joan, Karen, Marsha, and Chris were chatting when I entered. Chris, our receptionist, doubled as Jim's secretary. The rest of the group made up our human resource (HR) team. Unceremoniously, I grabbed one of the empty metal folding chairs and slid it over to their table. They were surprised by my presence and were ready to change the direction of the conversation, but I bid them to continue, content to relax and listen in.

I munched on a slab of bologna sandwiched between two slices of white bread, a bag of potato chips, and a can of Diet Coke all purchased from a vending machine. The conversation was a pleasant change of pace for me. Having recently been promoted to senior manager over the company's two-shift camera assembly operation, most of the conversations I dealt with during the day had to do with personnel problems, product quality issues, or schedule changes.

Marsha did most of the talking, or should I say bragging, as grandmothers tend to do. Her words carried the weight of hugs. When she injected her daughter's recent pregnancy into the conversation, it elevated the joy in the room several notches. During the course of the conversation, I learned that Marsha's daughter had a three-year-old grandson and a new puppy.

Marsha was a slender woman in her fifties about average height. She kept her gray hair short. Gold wire-rimmed glasses adorned a kind face. She continued talking with the ease of a storyteller, answering occasional questions from her captivated audience. The conversation took a sharp turn when her words darkened like storm clouds, threatening the umbrella of happy thoughts we all gathered under.

She was concerned about the physical and emotional load her daughter was carrying and wondered how she'd be able to handle another child in her life. Apparently, the little boy and his puppy amounted to quite a handful. Their lunch break ended abruptly when someone called everyone's attention to the time. I tarried for a while to finish my lunch, indulging myself with memories of baby Dan and Sheba.

The remaining days of summer passed quickly as I worked with HR to staff our camera assembly lines during the blitz of late-August vacations. Workers needed to maintain production quotas, and daily camera shipments needed to arrive on time. Occasionally, the lunchroom conversation regarding Marsha's daughter entered my mind. My thoughts, however, betrayed me. I wasn't concerned about Marsha's daughter or her grandson, for that matter. I wondered what would become of the puppy. I couldn't seem to get the little creature out of my mind, recalling how hard it was to let go of Sheba over a decade ago. What if they had to put the dog up for adoption? Should I casually offer to take the creature if it came to that?

When I returned to work after Labor Day, I could hardly believe my ears. Marsha was asking around the office if anyone wanted to adopt a puppy, the very same one occupying my thoughts. In passing, I inquired about what type of dog it was but gave her no indication of my interest. She described him as a black mutt that might have some retriever in him. Moments later, I sat at my desk busying my mind with scenarios that could require my involvement.

When I first proposed the idea of adding another dog to our family, Patty simply listened. She knew and understood me well. If she wasn't thrilled with the idea, she would patiently hear me out and then wait a few days until the idea passed. Many of my ideas did. This time, however, it did not pass—it festered like an infected wound. As a result, the subject found its way into more and more family conversations.

My wonderful idea did not come without opposition. Dan and Mike, now old enough to have intelligent conversations with us at the dinner table, reminded me that we already had a dog. Her name was Lady. I think they were concerned she might somehow be less loved or appreciated. I had to credit the boys for helping me see the irony of my situation. If another dog were to become part of the family, Dan and Mike still had their dog. My scheming, however, would break a bond Marsha's grandson had with his puppy.

I watched Lady following the boys around the house. Surely, she missed the days when she had their undivided attention. Our children were young men and always looking for an occasion to explore the outside world around them. Still, Dan and Mike never mistreated Lady or shooed her away from what they were doing. Had I considered what the addition of another dog would mean to her? Would Lady see a puppy as competition for our affection or a companion? The last thing I wanted was to make her feel unloved. I shook off a mental picture of her curled up in a corner, waiting out the remaining days of her life. Instead, I assured myself Lady could use the company. A puppy might even make her feel and act younger.

It was hard not to think of Sheba with this puppy up for adoption. I was determined not to let this golden opportunity pass if I could help it. You could say I went on the offensive. I began using "when" instead of "if" in my conversations regarding Lucky, the little puppy whom I now coveted. This subtle change did not go unnoticed. An eerie silence crept over our home when I brought up the subject of Lucky. I embraced the silence as a victory of sorts but decided to ease up when it became obvious I was trying too hard to impose my will. Was I really being that selfish? Maybe. But then I reasoned, *I've been taking care of the boys' dog for years, and I've asked for nothing in return.* I circled back to the idea of why this opportunity had been dropped right into my lap in the first place. Wasn't I supposed to act on it? The only person who really mattered to me on this issue was Patty. I knew I wouldn't be able to live with myself if she and I weren't in agreement.

"Babe, if you really want Lucky, then agree to take him," Patty said several days into my campaign, which caught me completely by surprise.

"I'm willing to forget about this whole thing if it's going to drive a wedge between us."

"Trust me, it won't. I've given it a lot of thought. You've been a terrific husband and father, and I am forever grateful for that."

"Should I worry about Dan and Mike? They don't seem thrilled with the idea."

"You aren't taking Lady away from them. Besides, you and I both know they'll probably be excited to have a puppy running around the house."

Part of me wondered if Patty was worried that I might be having a midlife crisis of some kind. Did she agree to let me have Lucky because she thought this was something she could handle? Whatever the reason, I knew bringing another dog into our house would cost her something. I cherished the thought of her being willing to compromise and have enough faith in me to make the right choice. Compromise and faith in each other were the glue that held our marriage together.

I had to temper the wave of excitement that rose within me when the prospect of owning Lucky suddenly became a legitimate possibility. Hopefully, I did not wait too long to express my interest. Like a child anticipating Christmas morning, I waited out the weekend for a chance to speak to Marsha. When I arrived at work, I remembered she was typically off on Mondays. Tuesday came and I was swamped with problems at work. It wasn't until Wednesday that I finally had a chance to speak to her. When I conveyed my interest to her, she practically jumped out of her shoes.

"Seriously, you'll take Lucky?"

"Yes, I've wanted another dog for a long time."

"You're the answer to our prayers!"

I hadn't anticipated this degree of enthusiasm. Was there a reason the family wanted to unload their dog so quickly? I decided I was just being paranoid. It was time to celebrate and prepare my family for Lucky's arrival.

I sat at my desk on the agreed-upon Friday in October, waiting for Marsha to arrive with Lucky. I was forty-one years old and had eclipsed what I considered to be the halfway point in my life. I guess you could say I was a "glass half empty" person. Try as I might, I couldn't convince myself otherwise. I saw evidence of my aging every time I looked in the mirror. My hairline was receding, creeping past my temples. Fortunately, I still had a thick patch of brown hair atop my head that I could comb in such a way as to hide it. My growing waistline bothered me most of all. I had gained twenty pounds since I left the factory floor to work behind a desk. I never used to worry about what I ate. Now, overeating joined a host of other things in life that came with consequences.

Until recently, I believed I was somehow immune to the aging process. But looking in the mirror every day convinced me otherwise. I always looked at the aging process as if it were a rut in the road of life that only others fell into. I assumed once you fell into one of these ruts, there was no getting out of it. Furthermore, it seemed to me that these ruts took you to undesirable destinations. I told myself

Lucky was just the sort of thing that would prolong my glory years and prevent a rut from claiming me.

The phone rang, piercing the silence like the starting bell of a horse race.

"Bill, Marsha's here," Chris said in a monotone voice.

"Thanks, tell her I'll be right there."

Adrenaline surged through my body. I scurried around my office, closing drawers and straightening the paperwork on my desk. Even in my haste, I felt obligated to comply with Jim's "clean desk" policy. I shoved my day planner in one pocket and my keys in the other and headed out the door.

I drew in a deep breath when I stepped out into the hallway, attempting to squash my enthusiasm. For some crazy reason, I subscribed to the notion that a person in management needed to appear reserved in the face of excitement. The more I tried to restrain the bounce in my step, the greater the joy that raged in my heart.

Chris, a tall thin woman in her late twenties, had shoulder-length auburn hair, a round freckled face, and maintained a dry sense of humor. She was in effect a sentry behind the reception desk ready to direct the path of visitors as they entered. Marsha stood in the waiting area chatting with Chris through an open window above the receptionist's desk. They interacted frequently during the work-week and to my knowledge never ran out of things to talk about. Today, however, Marsha played the role of visitor because she had taken the day off. Both ladies took visual aim at me when I approached.

"Are you leaving for the day?" Chris was required to ask.

"That depends whether or not Marsha brought Lucky."

"I did!"

"I guess I'm leaving then," I said with a chuckle.

The two comrades exchanged farewells as I passed through the doorway separating the reception area from the waiting room. Chris closed the window as we were leaving, trapping the words still tumbling out of her mouth behind a pane of glass.

"So, are you ready to meet Lucky?" Marsha asked.

"Yeah, but I'm feeling a little guilty that I'm taking him away from your grandson."

"He did mention something about you being his sworn enemy. But I wouldn't lose any sleep over it."

"Stop!" I said, breaking into a wide grin.

The late-afternoon sun hung low in the sky. We were immediately blinded by its brightness when we set foot in the parking lot. I shaded my eyes and breathed in the cool fall air. It smelled earthy. As if coerced by the aroma, a twenty-five-year-old memory surfaced. During a less complicated time in my life, my brothers and I loved to toss a football around in the front yard. "Tackle the guy with the football" we called it. Those were the days when all we cared about was playing outside until the sun set. We rolled around in the wet grass and dirt until Mom called us inside for supper.

"My keys are in here somewhere," Marsha said, jerking me back to the present.

"I'm not in any hurry."

"Here they are," she said, jingling them like a bell.

Marsha unlocked the rear hatch of her station wagon and lifted it slowly. I steeled myself, ready to grab Lucky should he try to make a break for it. To my surprise (and disappointment) the entire rear compartment was filled with brightly colored milk crates. Each bin was overflowing with papers or brochures of some kind. I saw no evidence of Lucky.

"Where's the dog?" I asked.

Unfazed, Marsha hunched forward and dragged a blue-and-white pet carrier out from among the crates. I'd seen this container before. Patty had one just like it that we transported our *cat* to the vet in.

"It's the only thing we could find to put him in."

"I imagined he would be bigger," I said.

Marsha looked at me and smirked.

"Do you know how long it took us to squeeze him into this thing?" she replied.

She released the latches, and a black snout pushed the door fully open. I looked on in amazement as a gangly creature slowly exited like a butterfly emerging from a cocoon. Moments later, the full frame of a five-month-old male Labrador Retriever stood before me.

"*This* is Lucky!" Marsha said, gesturing with a ceremonial flair.

She took a length of tattered-cotton clothesline and looped it around the puppy's neck. Lucky stood on the weathered asphalt, shaking out the kinks of his confinement. It was quite an elaborate ordeal. It started with his head, shaking it from side to side, then extended to his torso and finally to the very tip of his tail.

"How does that feel?" I asked.

The reality of what our acquaintance meant struck me as I held the length of rope. Two souls were joined together by a piece of clothesline. His jet-black coat glistened in the sunlight. The faint scent of baby shampoo teased my nostrils. I noticed he had many of the features one would expect to see in a Labrador Retriever: a square head, thick tail, and oversize webbed paws. The white-speckled patch of fur on his chest left no doubt of his mixed heritage. When two beautiful brown eyes looked up at me inquisitively, nothing else seemed to matter.

Marsha fetched a small pouch of veterinary papers from the front seat of her car while Lucky and I waited. The sound of rustling papers caught his attention. Perhaps he thought a dog treat of some kind might be forthcoming. I caught a glimpse of Marsha pressing a small white envelope into the packet of papers.

"It's a note for your wife. We're all very grateful that you're willing to take Lucky."

"We're happy to have him."

Marsha bent down and patted Lucky on the head.

"You be a good dog," she said, adding a sigh.

"Thank you again for bringing him here on your day off."

I could see the relief spreading across her face as she rose and headed back to her car.

Lucky and I lingered, and I politely waved good-bye. My companion seemed transfixed on a nearby insect and seemed totally unaware that a transfer of ownership had transpired. The frayed rope that guided him to me was about to take him in a completely new direction.

"Come on, Lucky, let's go home."

We ambled toward my blue Chevy Lumina van about a dozen parking spaces away. Lucky moved erratically, wandering left and right but pulling me in the general direction I wanted to go.

I opened the sliding door of the van and watched Lucky rocket through the opening. *That was easy,* I thought. Before I had fully processed the thought, horror engulfed me as I watched his progress abruptly halted. My new acquaintance strained against a taunt rope determined to continue. I thought it was odd that I didn't feel a similar strain on my arm. Looking down, I realized I no longer held the rope in my hand.

The sickening sound of Lucky gasping for air caused a wave of panic to ripple through me. The rope looped around his neck had become a hangman's noose. I scanned the van's interior and saw nothing but a sea of blue upholstery. Time slowed to a crawl as adrenaline coursed through my veins.

Focus! I need to focus!

Desperately, I scanned the van's interior again, forcing myself to be more deliberate, searching for anything out of the ordinary. Seconds passed. I grabbed the rope to take the pressure off his throat and traced it back to its origin. The rope had gotten snagged in an armrest. In anticlimactic fashion I lifted the armrest and freed the rope.

I hugged Lucky and rubbed his head and neck. While I enthusiastically comforted him, I removed the rope and tossed it toward the front of the van. I couldn't afford to have this happen again on the drive home. Lucky, realizing his freedom, escaped my embrace and bounded wildly from seat to seat. At least *he* wasn't emotionally damaged.

I made my way to the driver's seat, started the engine, and pointed the van toward home.

∾

Choosing

Most dog owners have "first encounter" stories or puppy memories they could share. The remainder of our pet's stay with us often plays out in ordinary fashion. While the days we spend with them may be ordinary, it's the bond between the dog and his or her owner that proves extraordinary. That special bond began with a choice. I chose Lucky after he became available for adoption. Plans were made to incorporate him into our family because I wanted to have a relationship with him like I once had with Sheba.

The idea of choosing something may seem like a superficial thing. That is until I consider that acting on my choices defines who I am as a person. For example, in choosing and adopting a dog, I become a pet owner.

Relationships are based on *mutual* choice, two individuals who choose each other. When I chose to offer my love to Lucky and he acted on the provisions I made for him, we had the makings of a relationship. We affirmed our relationship with love, devotion, and faithfulness. My future was altered when I made Lucky part of my life.

My relationship with God began in a similar fashion. He chose me (1 Peter 2:9–10) to have a relationship with him (2 Thessalonians 2:13–14). Once I accepted the provision He made for me (Romans 3:21–24), I began a relationship with Him. I affirmed my relationship with God by expressing my love, devotion, and faithfulness to Him. I chose to love God because I acted on His love for me (1 John 4:19). Having a relationship with God has altered my eternal destiny.

So why do I make choices? Whether I realize it or not, I make choices to express or exercise my will. I make mindless choices every day such as what I'm going to wear or what candy bar I'm going to buy out of a vending machine. I'd like to think the important choices I make are rational ones. Rational choices require information. Knowing, or foreknowledge, precedes these choices. This requires knowing or learning something about what I am choosing and, if necessary, determining what it will cost me (Luke 14:26–29).

I chose Lucky after I knew something about him and considered what it would cost our family.

God's choices are based on foreknowledge. He chose me before the world was ever created (Ephesians 1:4–5). Before I was formed in my mother's womb, God knew all about me (Jeremiah 1:5). But what did it cost God to choose me? It cost Him the death of his only Son, Jesus Christ (John 3:16–18) to enable me to have a relationship with him.

Mega choices are made with an intended plan or purpose in mind. The purpose connects me to the person or thing I am choosing and heightens my interest or desire for it. I chose Lucky for a host of personal reasons. I wanted to help the family who was unable to keep him. Patty and I had found ourselves on the opposite side of a similar situation almost twenty years earlier when we decided to give up our dog. I also hoped Lucky would fill the whole in my heart left by Sheba.

Just as I had a purpose or plan for Lucky, God had one for me. Part of God's plan involved gifting me in a unique way (1 Corinthians 1:4–9). Once I discovered my uniqueness, life began to make sense. Using my gifts and resources for God's purposes deepens my relationship with Him.

I used to wonder why God chose me and not somebody else. What made me so special? He didn't just choose me; he chose every-one. He desires that every person would enter into a relationship with Him (1 Timothy 2:4). Perhaps the better question is, "Why don't more people choose God?"

Even after knowing, careful planning, and then choosing, there is always an element of risk involved. Things may not turn out as planned. Lucky was no exception. I only knew what Marsha had told me about him and only listened to what I wanted to hear.

Fortunately, when God chose me, there was no gambling or risk involved. He already knew everything there was to know about me (1 John 3:20). He knew I wasn't perfect and that I would at some point fail Him. It is reassuring to know that nothing can separate me from His love (Romans 8:38–39).

But you are a chosen people, a royal priesthood, a holy nation, God's special possession, that you may declare the praises of him who called you out of darkness into his wonderful light. (1 Peter 2:9)

For he chose us in him before the creation of the world to be holy and blameless in his sight. (Ephesians 1:4)

Yet to all who did receive him, to those who believed in his name, he gave the right to become children of God—children born not of natural descent, nor of human decision or a husband's will, but born of God. (John 1:12–13)

EIGHT

A Surprising Welcome

THE TRIP HOME lasted fifteen minutes. My mind raced as I drove just over the thirty-five-mile-an-hour speed limit. I kept glancing down at the speedometer and repeatedly had to lighten my foot on the gas pedal. Euphoria overwhelmed me as I drove. Bringing Lucky home with me was a dream come true. I waited so long to have the kind of relationship with a dog I once had with Sheba.

A single thought rained on my happiness. *How will the rest of the family receive its newest member?* Introductions were minutes away, and I hoped the reception would be a friendly one.

I wasn't worried about Patty. She made it clear she was supportive of the idea. She loved animals as much as I did. I learned when we dated in college that we'd both wanted to be veterinarians when we were in grade school. Since the earliest days of our marriage, we'd always had a pet of some kind. Patty had a special affection for birds. She had a parakeet named Charlie and later a cockateel named Rusty. I had a thing for fish, having received a twenty-nine-gallon aquarium one Christmas from my parents. We always kept the tank stocked with fish until we had to empty it out for safety reasons. Mike, a toddler at the time, wouldn't stop playing on the lower shelf of the aquarium stand. It was an accident waiting to happen.

Instinctively, my foot bounced from the brake to the gas pedal when the motorist directly behind me honked his horn. It's a sad day on Planet Earth when lingering a couple of seconds at a traffic light after it turned green was sufficient grounds to raise the ire of trailing motorists. I looked over at Lucky and smiled. Nothing was going to sour my mood today.

I hoped Dan and Mike would be friendly to our newest family member. I'd lectured them on several occasions on the importance of making Lucky feel welcome. Patty thought the boys would be excited about having a puppy in the house again. I hoped she was right. However, Lady was the only dog ever to live in *this* house. Dan and Mike were very young when Lady came to live with us. She was the only dog they'd ever known.

One thing I thought I had going for me was the boys were entering their teen years. They'd discovered that visiting friends and being involved in extracurricular activities were more appealing than hanging around the house. Lady still held a special place in their hearts, but she'd be gone in a few years. I hoped they weren't too busy to realize that. Perhaps Lucky's arrival wouldn't be such a big deal to them after all.

No one greeted us when we pulled in the driveway. I doubt a point was being made, but the thought did cross my mind. The lack of fanfare afforded me the luxury of lingering in the quietness with my new friend. I wondered how I would remember this day years from now.

I shut off the engine and remained in my seat. Predictably, the world around me marched on. Electric lanterns fastened to the side of our house flickered erratically, teased by the shadows created by branches waving in an intermittent breeze. The maple trees themselves were skirted with colorful wreaths of leaves covering the ground around them. Birds conversed with one another in song. The clouds, painted red and purple by the setting sun, seemed to mourn the loss of the orb as the horizon consumed its prize. Red, orange, and yellow leaves continued to fall at random, drifting to the ground like parachutes.

The longer I sat, the more beautiful and peaceful the moment became. Soon boredom crept into the bones of my companion. He stood up and circled around the edges of the passenger seat before deciding to leap into my lap. The unfamiliar scents streaming in through a gap in the window proved to be too much for him to ignore. Lucky chased the scents with his wet nose, leaving long squiggly streaks on the glass.

I guess it was time to get moving, so I collared Lucky with the rope and gently poured him out of my lap and onto the asphalt driveway. He immediately stretched the cord taut, lured by the fragrance of the evergreen and holly bushes lining our sidewalk. Our progress, if you could call it that, slowed to a crawl as he sniffed and watered each bush.

Unceremoniously, I opened the front door and crossed the threshold. To my surprise, Lucky followed. I took this as a positive sign, but then again, the smell of supper emanating from the kitchen may have lured him inside.

"Hi, honey, we're home!"

Patty, working in the kitchen, left the stove and poked her head around the corner.

"How did things go with Marsha?"

"Better than I expected . . . right up until the moment Lucky almost choked himself to death getting into the van."

"Oh dear! Was Marsha there when it happened?"

"No, thank goodness."

Patty's beauty hadn't diminished since our college days. Her enchanting smile, the feature that originally drew me to her, was ever present. Her hazel eyes, gentle and warm, continued to stir the deepest recesses of my soul. As she approached, I found myself anticipating an exchange of pleasantries. I held her in my arms and felt my lips tingle when they touched hers. Though the greeting lasted only a moment, it was one of the highlights of my busy day.

"You poor puppy!" she said, bending down and taking Lucky's head in her hands. "He's a cutie!"

Lucky pressed against my leg for emotional support when the friendly stranger let go. A timer in the kitchen erupted, causing the abrupt movement of the stranger to startle him.

"Are Dan and Mike around?" I asked.

"They're downstairs playing with Legos," she replied, throwing the words back over her shoulder as she retreated to the kitchen.

Dan and Mike loved their Legos. It was one of the few childhood toys they had yet to outgrow. When a department store went out of business a couple of years back, Jim and I toured the empty retail space to see if we could salvage anything for company use. I ended up bringing home two large display bins, each measuring about four feet square. We used one right away to gather and sort laundry in the basement. The boys found a use for the other one. It became their "Lego Pit," accommodating all the blocks they'd accumulated from a half dozen or so Christmases. The sides were low enough for Dan and Mike to sit on with their feet buried ankle deep in tiny plastic blocks. From a practical standpoint, if the Legos were in the bin, they weren't on the floor being stepped on by bare feet.

When the boys heard the kitchen timer go off, they bounded up the basement stairs making enough noise to wake the dead.

"Mom, I'm hungry," Mike whined.

"Is it time to eat yet?" Dan added.

"No, not yet," she answered.

"Hey, Dad brought Lucky home!" Mike said, suddenly noticing us standing in the entryway.

They immediately dashed in my direction. Mike dropped to his knees and skidded across the tile floor, barreling into Lucky.

"Easy, Mike, you'll scare him," I said.

Mike grabbed Lucky around the neck and tugged on him zealously. Our newest family member defended himself by pushing his muzzle into the face of the annoying human. He licked Mike aggressively, a move that sent the child tumbling backward onto his butt. Mike laughed.

Dan trailed a few feet behind his younger brother. His welcome was more subdued. He held out his hand for Lucky to sniff before wrapping his arms around the dog's neck and employing a cheek-to-cheek hug.

I'd been outspoken these past few days about the importance of making Lucky feel welcome. The boys were coached about being loving and kind, just as my parents had taught me. My parents fostered the belief that a loving heart enables relationships to flourish, while hostility can suffocate them.

What I observed constituted being loving and kind, but I also wondered if Lucky had the cute-puppy factor working. Nonetheless, it was a satisfying thing to witness. Over the years, I'd noticed that children seem to take to puppies like hydrogen atoms take to oxygen atoms to form a water molecule. Once the bond is formed, it is very hard to separate.

Having fulfilled their duty, the boys bounded off. Lucky's instincts suggested giving chase, but the strain of the rope against his neck provided immediate feedback to the contrary. Their sudden flight struck me as odd, but I certainly wasn't complaining.

A noticeable calmness fell over the entryway in the wake of their departure. I took a deep breath and slowly blew air out through my mouth, causing my cheeks to bulge. No doubt a habit dating back to my trumpet playing days. Reaching down, I patted my new companion on the head and spoke to him in soothing tones. I recruited a hanger from the hall closet that was willing to take the burden of my coat. After loosening my tie, I turned my attention to my shoes. Lucky looked on curiously. I wonder what dogs find so special about a human's shoes. I remembered how fanatical Sheba became whenever my hands touched them. Would Lucky react the same way in the days ahead?

"Welcome to your new home, Lucky," I said.

I finished separating my tie from my collar and removed my socks. It never ceased to amaze me how refreshed my bare feet felt when they pressed against the cool ceramic floor tiles. I was looking forward to spending a wonderful quiet weekend getting to know

Lucky. There were so many things I hoped we could do together, and I was already anticipating the fun we would have.

Suddenly, I heard the back door burst open in the kitchen with such force that it slammed against the pantry door behind it. The troubling scratching sound of claws searching for traction on the ceramic tile floor followed. Then I heard Patty yell, "Hey, get back here."

Though I couldn't see what was happening in the kitchen, I knew trouble was headed my way. I heard a low growl that grew in intensity. Lady was coming for Lucky. From the pounding of feet striking the floor, I knew Dan and Mike were not far behind. Patty, transferring macaroni from a pan into a baking dish, didn't have a free hand to intervene with. Given the combined length of our kitchen and dining area, the "welcome party" would reach us in a matter of seconds.

Lucky didn't seem concerned at first. Perhaps he thought the boys had returned for another round of fun. He rocked back and forth on his paws and wagged his tail excitedly. His posture changed the moment a mass of black-and-white fur streaked into view. Lady, traveling too fast to make a ninety-degree turn, broadsided the kitchen wall with a thud. Somehow her momentum kept her upright.

One thing I had learned over the years, Lady was very protective of our sons. The sight of a stranger invading our home seemed to enrage her. I watched the hair along the ridge of her back rise when she barked. I've known Lady all her life, and I'd never seen her act that way in front of me. Her display of rage, or whatever else you'd call it, was very intimidating. She barreled down the short hallway straight for us.

Lucky, now sensing danger, encircled me, wrapping the rope around my legs. At the last moment he dove between my legs, effectively hog-tying me. I did my best to keep my body between the two animals and credit the death grip I had on the stair railing with keeping me upright. Bobbing and weaving with my feet lashed together, I felt like I was performing a yet-to-be-named dance number.

Lady gave me a confused look when I screamed at her and pushed her away. My instruction for her to go lie down was being ignored, however. Out of the corner of my eye I caught a glimpse of a gray creature hurrying in the direction of the basement. Kit, our cat, was momentarily drawn to the scene by all the excitement, then, thinking the better of it, decided to head for the basement.

Dan and Mike arrived on the scene immediately after Lady. Their mouths gaped like stooges as they skated into the arena in their stockinged feet. In truth, the whole incident resembled a *Three Stooges* episode. My participation certainly qualified me as the third stooge.

"What were you guys thinking?" I demanded.

"Dad, we were just trying to help," Dan responded, clearly in shock.

"Help? How is *this* being helpful?"

"We wanted Lady to meet Lucky," Mike said. His lips began to quiver, and tears welled up in his eyes. "Honest!"

"Okay, okay," I said, recalibrating my disappointment to what now seemed more akin to a childish blunder. "Dan, will you please grab hold of Lady and take her back out to the garage?"

Patty stood behind the boys observing everything.

"I thought I told you to keep Lady in the garage," she said, pausing to let the words sink in. "What do you have to say to your father?"

Two independent sighs produced a unified response, "Sorry, Dad."

"It's not that I don't appreciate you trying to help. Next time, please wait for me to ask for it."

Dan hung his head and led his dog back to the garage, following the direction of Patty's pointing finger.

"Mike, come over here, buddy. Daddy's sorry for yelling. Will you hang on to Lucky for me so I can go change?"

Mike's sniffles ceased when I handed him the rope. He wiped away the tears with the back of his hand. A smile spread across his face as he headed into the living room proudly escorting Lucky.

There was still a gap between his age and his maturity. Junior high school was not far away. He was a very sensitive child, and I hoped he'd be ready in time. I looked forward to seeing the man he'd become.

When I headed down the hallway, I noticed the armpits of my dress shirt were soaked through, the aftereffect of warding off a potential disaster. When I clutched the bedroom doorknob, I began to anticipate the soothing effect a change of clothes would offer. As I changed out of my work clothes, the manager in me immediately began to strategize how I would get Lucky and Lady to peacefully coexist. No ideas were forthcoming. They had to get along or Lucky would have to go back. Slipping on a pair of jeans and a T-shirt had a soothing effect on my entire body. Moments later, I emerged from the bedroom a new person.

Lucky was now in our home, and I was determined to begin a new life with him.

I heard Patty call out, "Supper's ready!"

Welcoming

Most people have an internal desire to be loved, feel needed, and be included in the world around them. But they also possess an inherently selfish nature. If attention is going to be dispensed, it seems quite natural to position themselves on the receiving end of it. Why, then, should a person be so eager to offer hospitality to someone else when they can hardly get enough attention themselves? The Bible offers this assertion: "love your neighbor as yourself" (Leviticus 19:18; Matthew 22:39).

I have seen persons appear to be loving and welcoming toward others but with selfish motives. I walked this tightrope when I sought to bring Lucky into my life. He was going to be *my* dog. I risked alienating members of my family for my own selfish gain. My family, on the other hand, unselfishly welcomed Lucky.

Hostility, indifference, and selfishness are the enemies of hospitality and can suffocate a relationship. A welcoming spirit, however, has the opposite effect. Perhaps dog lovers bond so quickly with their pets because of the welcoming spirit their canines possess. I am reminded of this every time Lucky approached me with his tail wagging.

How, then, does one become more welcoming? Experience tells me, though it is expressed *outwardly*, hospitality is cultivated *inwardly*. It's an attitude of the heart rooted in humility (Romans 12:2, 3, 16). When I think of humility, it invokes a notion of surrender and vulnerability. Not everyone can relate to that. But how can I expect someone to get to know me better if all I do is offer them silence or insult or ignore them? Whenever I struggle with the thought of being humble, I need only to remind myself that God shows favor to the humble and guides them (Psalm 25:9; Proverbs 3:34).

Am I making too big a deal out of this idea of welcoming? I don't think so. Consider that a welcoming spirit is paramount to pursuing a relationship with God. After choosing to enter a relationship with Him, the next all-important step is to welcome God into all areas of your life (Luke 10:27). How can you expect to have access to God if you refuse Him access to yourself?

When I entered a relationship with Jesus, He placed his Spirit within me as a seal, or deposit, guaranteeing my inheritance of eternal life (Ephesians 1:13–14). This same Spirit longed to be my advocate and companion on my journey through life (John 14:16). He came from God and works for God. The work of the Spirit includes pointing out things I should or shouldn't do so I can maintain a healthy relationship with God. The Holy Spirit also helps me understand God's plan for my life (John 14:26). The Spirit of God dwelling in me helps keep me aligned with God's will. When this happens, a change occurs, and I become less selfish and more loving.

Hospitality, or welcoming, is one of the hallmarks of Jesus' earthly ministry (Matthew 11:28–30). His New Testament teachings revolve around the command, "love one another" (Matthew 5:43–44;

22:39). Going out of my way to be friendly to someone is an *outward* demonstration of an *inward* obedience to God (Romans 12:10, 13). I sometimes need to remind myself that my obedience to God should be motivated by the unmerited kindness and generosity I have already received from Him (Luke 6:35–36). My two sons welcomed Lucky out of obedience to their earthly father.

Though it's hard for me to fully grasp, there are people on this earth with a special gift of hospitality. They seem to accomplish it with so little effort as if it's part of the fiber of their being (Romans 12:8). For these individuals, hospitality is a gift, a special talent, given by the Holy Spirit. Any spiritual gift, including hospitality, must be dispensed in such a way as to reflect God's love. Without love, God's gifts accomplish nothing (1 Corinthians 13:1–13). Patty is clearly gifted in the realm of hospitality.

A welcoming spirit is evidence of God working in a person's heart. Our faith in God should shine like a light to the world around us. People can't see God directly, but they can see God's love radiating from the lives of those who know Him personally.

Does the fragrance of God's love cover my awkward attempts to show hospitality to others? This thought forces me to consider my motives as I attempt to be more welcoming. It also reminds me to consider the needs of others before considering my own.

Love is patient, love is kind. It does not envy, it does not boast, it is not proud. (1 Corinthians 13:4)

Above all, love each other deeply, because love covers over a multitude of sins. Offer hospitality to one another without grumbling. Each of you should use whatever gift you have received to serve others, as faithful stewards of God's grace in its various forms. (1 Peter 4:8–10)

Don't forget to show hospitality to strangers, for by so doing some

people have shown hospitality to angels without knowing it.
(Hebrews 13:2)

NINE

The Note

PATTY PREPARED MACARONI and cheese for dinner that evening. Everyone in our family loved it; consequently, we ate it a lot. It was far tastier than the boxed variety of noodles with powdered or liquified cheese. Her version consisted of a mixture of grated sharp cheddar cheese, milk, and other ingredients that were melted to form a sauce and poured over cooked noodles before baking it to perfection.

Before I sat at the table, I made sure both dogs were leashed in separate areas so they couldn't see each other. From my seat, I observed Lucky lying quietly in the entryway by the front door. Lady sat impatiently on an area rug leashed to the doorknob at the far end of the kitchen. She wasn't used to being restrained while we ate and kept a wary eye on the proceedings. If scraps were going to be doled out at the end of the meal, she intended to be first in line. The newcomer would have to wait.

The chaos of finding our seats around the dinner table gave way to reverent anticipation as we waited for Patty to place supper on the table. Wisps of steam rose from the glass dish containing the baked macaroni and cheese. She placed a second dish of brightly colored peas beside it. The two dishes combined to generate a pleasing aroma, which hung in the air. Beads of moisture formed capillaries on the outside of our drinking glasses filled with ice water.

I bowed my head and began to pray, "God is great, God is good . . ."

Everyone joined in to help me finish the prayer. As a family we had prayed this prayer together more times than I could count. Yes, the words were childish, but to the four of us seated around the table it served to remind us of how blessed we were as a family. I hoped we would never get to the point where we took for granted any meal that was placed before us.

"Amen."

At our table, eating took precedence over conversation at mealtime. We were fast eaters. To hesitate or err on the side of conversation could cost you a chance to completely satisfy your appetite. Talk flowed more freely once the supply of food had dwindled. When guests joined us for a meal, the process was altered. This caused a unique form of stress brought on by slowing down the pace of the meal for conversation's sake.

I guess you could say I was the one responsible for creating this environment. I grew up in a family of five children where money was tight. As a result, my mother used every means at her disposal to stretch the food we did have. She did things like adding powdered milk and water to regular milk, making it a fifty-fifty mixture. Pizza night consisted of one or two slices of homemade pizza and all the popcorn you could eat. To commemorate that occasion, she served orange juice that was watered-down with Kool-Aid. I was raised on a steady diet of casseroles and stews, all of which left a warm, lingering feeling in my stomach. To this day, "warm and gooey" casserole dishes remain a favorite of mine.

Stretching out the food supply was only half the battle. Ensuring every child had access to a portion of the food required diligence on the part of both parents. When we were old enough to put a helping of food on our own plate under the watchful eyes of our parents, we were expected to eat all of it—even if it was turnips mistaken for squash. We were routinely lectured on the number of less fortunate children all around the world who were starving.

When all five children had a plate of food, the three oldest siblings (of whom I was one) had a secret understanding which I called "the early bird gets the worm" rule. If you were among the first to eat everything on your plate, a second helping of your favorite dish was available on a "first come, first served" basis. Unknowingly, my parents created an eating competition. The stakes were high, and unlike the Olympic games, finishing third rarely qualified you for a prize. It wasn't until after I married that I realized that food tasted better when it was savored.

"Dad, what are we doing this weekend?" Dan asked over the clatter of forks.

"I thought we'd spend time with Lucky."

"The *whole* weekend?" Mike said, making himself heard.

"Lucky needs to learn our routine."

"It's just *one* weekend," Patty added.

"*Mom!*" Mike whined, as if pleading for the reversal of an unjust verdict.

"Hey, I almost forgot. Marsha included a note with Lucky's vet papers," I said.

Springing up from the table, I retrieved the note from the pouch of papers still residing in my coat. Patty, a thank-you-note writer herself, would undoubtedly appreciate receiving one. I handed her the note and retreated to my chair watching expectantly for her reaction. I was caught completely off guard when her face began to sour.

"Bill, this isn't a thank-you note—it's a warning."

"What are you talking about?"

"It describes what Lucky did to their mudroom. He ripped up chunks of their linoleum floor and chewed through some of the drywall." She glanced down at our oak dinette set before continuing. "He gnawed on the legs of their table and chairs."

"Let me see that," I said, believing she had fabricated the words.

"Bill, he's a monster!"

"He doesn't *look* like a monster. Besides, it's not like we can take him back. I promised Marsha we'd take care of him."

"Didn't she say anything to you about this? She must have mentioned something!"

"She mentioned that he chews—but all puppies will chew!"

We were quickly heading past the point of neutral conversation like a train charging headlong into a dark tunnel. The outcome of the conversation would remain in doubt until the engine reemerged on the other side.

"Dan, why don't you and Mike take the dogs out into the garage? And while you're out there, take Lucky out into the dog pen to see if he needs to go to the bathroom. Come and get me if the dogs start fighting," I said.

To my amazement both creatures seemed amicable toward one another and exited the kitchen without incident. It took some convincing for Lady to leave because the smell of the macaroni and cheese still hung in the air. I found myself wishing I was taking the dogs outside instead of the boys. Patty and I resumed our conversation after everyone made their exit.

"We can't leave that dog alone in this house," Patty said, waving the note in the air for emphasis.

"What other choice do we have?"

"What about that dog crate you talked about getting."

"I think I said, 'If we needed to, I'll get one.'"

"I don't think there's any doubt about that now, do you?"

"All right, I'll look into it."

"I think you should get one tonight. I promise not to harp on how much it costs; I'll leave that up to you. Just make sure you bring one home with you."

Patty's words were calm and direct. She rarely had to raise her voice when she talked to me because she knew me so well. Besides, she was in the right, and we both knew it.

"Can you look after Lucky while I'm gone?"

"You're taking him with you. I need to get the house ready."

"Ready for what?"

"The dog crate."

Patty didn't resent Lucky coming here. She'd put up with numerous pets over the years: cats, dogs, birds, fish, a turtle, and some hamsters. In my overwhelming desire to possess Lucky, I didn't ask enough questions and was willing to overlook any potential warning flags because I wanted him so badly. The note's telling words spoiled his otherwise delightful introduction into our home. The indictment immediately changed our perception of him. We needed to start things off on the right foot if Lucky's stay with us was going to amount to anything. In Patty's eyes, success equated to keeping our house as intact as possible.

After a pregnant pause, Patty looked into my eyes and said, "I love you."

Translation: she considered the matter properly addressed and was already preparing to make the best of the situation.

"I love you too," I responded, making certain my heart captured the meaning of the words as they rolled off my tongue.

Patty and I got up and began gathering the dishes off the table. I was left with the feeling that our emotional attachment to one another had not been damaged. I thanked God silently for that feeling and for sending Patty into my life to be my companion. We understood each other's shortcomings. Neither of us was perfect, but our willingness to try to understand where the other was coming from had gotten us through some tough situations.

"I'd better go check on the boys," I said, suddenly remembering I'd sent them out without coats or shoes.

Lady trotted over to greet me when I entered the garage. She seemed satisfied with a simple pat on the head. I could hear the kids' voices, but Patty's car blocked my view. I veered around the car and followed the sound of their voices.

"Mike, why are you lying on the floor?"

Two years younger than his brother, Mike was covered in whatever residue had settled on the garage floor. The awkwardness of adolescence gripped his growing body. His reddish hair and round face gave him a jovial look. He peered up at me through sweat-fogged glasses.

"We're showing Lucky how to use the doggy door," he replied.

"Hi, Dad," Dan interjected, sticking his head through the opening.

"Where's the rest of you?" I asked, trying hard not to laugh at the talking head minus a body.

"I'm outside with Lucky."

"I can see that, but what are you doing out there?"

"Lucky was afraid to use the doggy door just like Lady was."

Already ultra thin, Dan's body seemed to thin further with each inch he gained in height. Very much the conversationalist, the glasses on his face gave him the appearance of a budding scientist. His smile, more reserved than his brother's, effectually hid the braces in his mouth.

"Dad, watch this," Mike said. "Here, Lucky! Here, Lucky!"

Mike lifted the clear plastic flap to show Lucky where he was, and then lowered it. He rapped on the wall for encouragement. This of course brought Lady running over to Mike and created a traffic jam at the opening Lucky was trying to pass through. We all laughed. Once Lady was corralled, Lucky was able to make his way through the opening and into the garage. The two dogs circled and sniffed each other.

"Nice job, guys. Now, go inside and grab your coats and shoes. We're going for a ride."

"Where are we going?" Mike asked, hoping the outing would include some form of kid-friendly entertainment.

"To the pet store."

"Cool," he replied.

"We need to get moving before the store closes. Remember to check your feet before you come inside."

"What for?" Dan asked.

"You were outside in the dog pen. Mom won't like it if you track dog poop into the house."

"That's disgusting," Dan said as they both giggled.

Several minutes later, Dan, Mike, Lucky, and I were driving down the highway headed west to a town called Brockport, once a frequent stop for barges traveling along the Barge Canal. Going to the store on a Friday evening with kids in tow was not how I'd imagined my relaxing weekend would begin. Thankfully, I already knew which store would have dog crates. Jim and I had recently toured a mail order company that sold merchandise for dogs. They allowed us to take a good look at their sophisticated conveyor system. We were always on the lookout for ways to improve the efficiency of our company. The company also had a retail store for its local customers.

A glowing neon "Open" sign greeted us as I pulled into the parking lot. The absence of cars brightened my mood. That meant I probably wouldn't have to stand in the checkout line very long. My objective was clear: secure a dog crate. Patty's instruction was even clearer: don't come home without one.

"Dan, I need you to stay in the van with your brother and Lucky."

"Why can't we come in with you?" Dan asked.

"I don't want to leave Lucky alone in the car."

"How come?" my young scientist inquired.

"Weren't you listening when Mom read the note about Lucky?"

Both children fell silent, which I could only guess meant their imaginations were running wild.

"Lock the doors and honk the horn if you need me. This shouldn't take long."

When I stepped inside, I immediately spotted a towering display of pet crates at the rear of the store. You could say it was my lighthouse, offering to guide me safely to my destination.

My exuberance waned when I arrived at the base of the monument and saw a sign attached to the display that read, "Please ask a store associate for assistance."

The manager in me interpreted the sign to mean my hopes for a quick transaction rested on the availability of some low-ranking store employee forced to work on a Friday evening while the more experienced staff had already started their weekend. I chuckled to myself in disbelief. Would the store associate I'd likely encounter know anything about the crates, or would I have to follow him or her around the store until they found someone who could help?

I searched the area adjacent to the display hoping to find a crate I could immediately take up to the checkout counter, but there weren't any. For a moment, I considered unstacking some of the smaller crates to gain access to a larger one, but I thought the better of it. It would take longer to explain to the store's security personnel why I was tampering with their display than it would to find an associate to assist me. Besides, if I got into trouble, Dan would take great pleasure in telling his mother all about it.

"Can I help you?" a voice behind me asked.

"Excuse me," I said, turning around.

"Is there something I can help you with?"

"I need one of these wire cages."

"I can help you with that. Did you have a particular style or size in mind?"

"I need something big and very strong," I said, immediately wishing I had chosen a more intelligent response.

"When you say 'strong,' are you referring to its overall construction or perhaps one with dual-reinforced latches on the door?"

"We have a Labrador Retriever," I replied, using the dog's breed like a password hoping it would grant me access to what I needed.

"Well then, this is the enclosure you should consider. It's made of heavy-gauge wire and has a double latching-door mechanism. Notice the one-piece plastic tray, which pulls out for easy cleaning."

I felt my face flush. I'm sure I would come to appreciate all these features eventually, but I wasn't in the mood to listen to a marketing spiel on a Friday night when I should be home relaxing in my favorite chair. But I bit my lip and let him continue. It would do me no good to insult a well-meaning employee who was just trying to be helpful.

"*And* it comes fully assembled," he said, smiling as he finished his presentation.

"It's not going to fit in my van," I blurted out, certain of my situation.

He assured me that it would and disappeared into the stockroom before I could convince him otherwise. The dog crate he showed me had to be three feet wide, three feet high, and four feet long. There was no way it would fit in our van without taking out some of the seats. *Why didn't I think about removing the rear seats before I left? What if I removed some of the seats and left them here and came back for them tomorrow?* I was in the process of convincing myself to do just that when the associate returned with a six-inch-thick crate on his cart. I felt my stature shrink measurably because it was clear the young man did know what he was talking about after all. Wasn't there something in the Bible about pride going before a fall? I found myself suddenly being grateful and appreciative of the young man's time. He was even kind enough to demonstrate how the pen could be erected in less than a minute.

"I'll take it!"

~

The Note

When I think of a handwritten note, pleasant thoughts usually come to mind. Such a note might be used to commemorate a special occasion such as a birthday, anniversary, holiday, or simply to say thank you. Notes can also be written to help us keep track of people, places, or events. They can be both positive and negative, a means of creating a permanent record.

The note about Lucky's negative behavior caught us off guard. That simple card was powerful evidence that would be used to incriminate him were it a trial in a court of law. It changed our opinion of him before we even got a chance to know him.

The lady who wrote the note did so because she felt obligated to warn us. There was no hiding the fact that Lucky had damaged their home. Yes, the damage was done when he was younger, and some might simply brush off this behavior as juvenile, a stage most puppies eventually grow out of. I had to support Patty's opinion on this matter, however. The truth regarding Lucky's past sins would follow him indefinitely. Patty considered the note in a loving manner and then took the appropriate action to protect our home. Her concern regarding Lucky's ability to damage the objects around him might someday play out as fact.

The words scribbled on the card were a permanent stain. Even if the ink faded over time or the note was lost, the condemning words would always remain. As his new family, we could not erase the past, but we hoped to prevent it from happening in the future, hence the pet enclosure. I hoped that once I got to know him better and built a relationship with him, his behavior might change.

When I look back over my life, I recognize that I've committed my share of wrongs in my youth. It would be an uncomfortable thought to imagine someone capturing every transgression in writing, especially the ones my parents never found out about. How would I react if such a document were shown to people who knew me? To say I would be embarrassed and humiliated would be an understatement. I would be forced to deny the transactions ever happened or endure the shame. Another option would be to pose excuses to justify my actions.

Many years have passed since the days of my youth. Am I a better person today? I'd like to think so. I have matured, taken on many responsibilities, and involved myself in honorable pursuits. But maturity, responsibility, accountability, and philanthropy have done nothing to deal with the stain of any past offenses. If I never reconciled these previous issues with God, they would still exist. In fact, if I add any recent mistakes, unruly thoughts, bad attitudes, selfish motives, etc., my condition wouldn't seem to have improved at all. From experience, I know that even "good" churchgoing people commit egregious offenses, even if only in their hearts or minds. The truth is, we have all fallen short of the perfect standard required to enter a relationship with God (Romans 3:23). These offenses, sins, or whatever we choose to call them act as a barrier separating us from

God. Without a permanent solution to this condition, we cannot hope to live beyond the grave in a place we call heaven.

Any potential solution to this predicament must reconcile not only past offenses but any future ones as well. Thankfully, God offers a perfect solution expressly for the whole of mankind in the person of His Son, Jesus Christ (John 3:16). Jesus is *the* permanent, everlasting solution, guaranteeing that my transgressions, if I confess them to Him, will be reconciled before God (John 3:18; Romans 8:1–2). Redemption, then, is not achieved through religious practices, but a rational choice made to enter a personal relationship with God by acknowledging the redemptive act of his Son, Jesus. Jesus died on the cross in our place to pay the required price for our sins.

No religious ritual can earn God's favor in this regard (Ephesians 2:8–9). Instead, I must acknowledge the existence of my sinful condition, believe that Jesus is God's Son, that He died for my sins and rose from the grave just as the Scriptures say (1 Corinthians 15:1–4). It's my confession, and my belief that Jesus is who He says He is, that declares me right with God. Jesus is the bridge between the certainty of my physical death and a glorious, resurrected life on the other side of death (Romans 6:23).

In this "saved" condition I am not left to travel through life on my own. I can approach God by talking directly to Him. Furthermore, God has given me three important resources: His Spirit to guide me (John 14:16–17), His written Word (the Bible), and the fellowship of other believers.

I have come to think of the Bible as God's personal note to me. His written word will never become outdated and can be viewed as the ultimate source of truth (Hebrews 4:12). It explains how much He loves me (Romans 5:8). His words hold the promise of a new home (John 14:1–3), an eternal existence (John 11:25–26), new relationships with other believers (Romans 12:4–5), and someday a new body free from defects (Philippians 3:20–21). These same scriptures tell me that God is constantly at work in my life, ensuring that everything that happens to me is for His greater good—including the things I don't understand (Romans 8:28).

My relationship with Lucky began with a simple desire for him. I welcomed him into my home and provided for his needs. Lucky responded by choosing to rely fully on me. He grew to crave my love and attention. I gave him gifts I knew he would love. He accepted them with great joy—as if they were the greatest gifts ever offered. In turn, I am delighted to be the object of his love and devotion.

My relationship with Lucky is easy enough to describe. But how do I describe my relationship with God? Do I desire Him as much as Lucky desires me. Do I crave His love and affection like Lucky craves mine? Just as I have demonstrated a desire to provide for Lucky, God will demonstrate His ability to provide for me. Do I long to be near God? Do I trivialize the gifts He has given me? I need to remember that God delights in my love and devotion.

For God so loved the world that he gave his one and only Son, that whoever believes in him shall not perish but have eternal life. (John 3:16)

By this gospel you are saved, if you hold firmly to the word I preached to you. Otherwise, you have believed in vain . . . that Christ died for our sins according to the Scriptures, that he was buried, that he was raised on the third day according to the Scriptures. (1 Corinthians 15:2–4)

Then I acknowledged my sin to you and did not cover up my iniquity. I said, "I will confess my transgressions to the LORD." And you forgave the guilt of my sin. (Psalm 32:5)

TEN

There's No Place Like Home

WHILE THE BOYS and I were out shopping, Patty stayed home to tackle the interior design challenge about to be created with the arrival of a dog crate. She had no idea of the size of the crate I was bringing home from the store. Still, she forged ahead evaluating each room in the house, looking for a sizable amount of underutilized space. If space was the primary concern, the decor, making it look like it belonged in a room, ran a close second.

We abandoned our "Noah's ark" decor years ago. Aquariums no longer lined the walls of our living room, and birdcages no longer hung from the ceiling. Patty put considerable effort into matching paint schemes with room furnishings. A brand-new crate, despite its gleaming appearance, was not about to change that.

Mike's bedroom quickly surfaced as the most likely candidate. His room was centrally located on the main floor and out of the immediate view of guests. Unfortunately for Mike, he wasn't present to hear all the advantages of placing it in his room, especially the one that included a new roommate.

"What do you mean he's staying in my room?" Mike barked when he heard the news.

"It's the best place in the house for him," Patty replied resolutely.

"What about Dan's room? His room is bigger than mine."

"Dan's bedroom is in the basement. That won't work."

"Take it easy, Mike, and don't talk to your mother like that," I cautioned.

"It's not fair!" Mike said, crossing his arms over his chest and forcing his trademark exaggerated pout.

"Mom went to a lot of trouble to figure this out. Let's just give it a try and see how it works out," I said, fully aware that any problems involving Lucky circled back to me.

"You won't even notice it's there because I'm going to camouflage it," Patty said.

Mike regained much of his composure at the mention of the word *camouflage* being of the age where anything to do with the military grabbed his interest.

I lugged my prize into the bedroom eager to show off how easily it assembled. With my audience looking on, I raised the middle section consisting of the four connected panels: top, bottom, left, and right. Together they form a three-dimensional rectangle. Then, one at a time, I raised the two end panels. Voilà, the dog pen was erected.

"It's so . . . big!" Patty commented as her smile forced me to laugh.

"Dad, it looks like a jail cell," Dan added.

"Or a circus cage!" Mike said.

Each comment incited more laughter. As much as I hated to admit it, they were right. We all had a good laugh. It seems the ice was broken, and we were ready to forge ahead.

Following Patty's direction, I slid the pen into the corner of the room. She went to work, producing a white Formica panel pillaged from somewhere in the basement and placed it atop the pen. It was nearly a perfect fit. The final step involved pushing Mike's bed up against it. Every side of the dog enclosure was now hidden except the front panel containing the door.

But Patty wasn't finished. Her eyes drifted over to the pile of stuffed animals on the floor. On most days Mike's creatures littered his room. The flat surface atop the pen would now be a gathering place for all his stuffed companions. I imagined a smile appearing on Patty's face when her idea for the stuffed animals first materialized.

Puppies, like children, have an inner curiosity that drives them to explore new and interesting things. Dan, Mike, and Lucky entered the shadowy interior of the pet enclosure. It was big enough to be a fort any kid would love to play in. Lady rested quietly in the opposite corner of the room resting her head on her front paws, content to observe the goings on. Dan and Mike called out trying to entice her to join them, but without success. Lady knew a trap when she saw one, having been confined far too many times in makeshift forts over the years.

I sat on the floor observing how the boys validated Patty's creative effort by spontaneously cramming themselves into the dog pen with Lucky. All my grumbling about having to go to the store on a Friday evening suddenly seemed meaningless. Lucky now had a place he could call home.

As the evening wound down, the boys made their way to their bedrooms. Lady followed Dan down the stairs to his room, which was her usual practice. Mike, nearly asleep already, staggered into his room and collapsed in his bed. With the evening's drama having reached a conclusion, I grabbed my coat and the royal blue leash I'd purchased to match his new collar. I was not about to let a black puppy roam free in the dark. Lucky followed me into the kitchen where we passed through a sliding glass door and made our way out onto the deck.

Carlin and I had constructed the two-tiered deck a few years after Patty and I bought the house. The larger of two decks was twenty feet by twelve feet and ran the entire length of the kitchen and dining area. It intersected a smaller ten-foot square deck which was eight inches lower. The lower deck housed our hot tub and could also be accessed from the garage. I installed a gate on the lower deck to serve as a sentry, protecting the hot tub from anyone climbing up the stairs from the backyard.

Lucky and I stepped out into the night. The darkness seemed impenetrable as we transitioned from the artificial light of the kitchen. Wary of his surroundings, Lucky pressed against my leg. I paused to give my eyes time to adjust to the darkness. A moment or two later I noticed thin strands of light bleeding out from the edges of the vertical blinds. This strange pattern of light caused the outdoor furnishings littering the deck to cast long, eerie shadows. The shadows exaggerated the exact placement of each object. I probed my way across the mayhem to the certainty of the dog-eared fence boards that served as a railing rimming the perimeter of the deck. Lucky followed tightly behind me. My hand passed over the boards one by one as I made my way toward the gate.

Caught up in the overall success of Lucky's first day with us, I allowed the familiarity of my surroundings to trump precaution. The eight-inch step down to the lower deck came sooner than I expected. In an instant the serenity of the night was shattered. The misstep cost me my balance and sent me crashing against the hot tub. Were it not for the padded cover, I would have gone swimming. Lucky, spooked by the commotion, sprinted in the opposite direction, and collided with a deck chair, causing him to let out a yelp. I regained my balance and tried to gather my wits about me.

"Come here, Lucky," I said in a soothing tone. "It's okay."

Cautiously, I made my way to Lucky, snapped on his leash, and consoled him. Not wanting to repeat my tumbling experience, Lucky and I carefully navigated the stairs downward and onto the slippery wet grass. The backyard became featureless in the darkness as we moved away from the house. It also made Lucky invisible.

After Lucky finished his business, we retraced our steps, and I sank into one of the swiveling deck chairs. Though I was tired from all the excitement the day brought, a part of me didn't want the day to end. It was a perfect day, one I had longed for.

I coaxed Lucky up into my lap and rocked him gently. As I gazed heavenward, I noticed that more and more stars became apparent, filling in the gaps between the brighter ones. They were a perfect mixture of peace and beauty. I now understood why some people were so enamored with stargazing.

It seemed that whenever I made time to sit quietly, work found a way to intrude upon my thoughts. I laughed to myself as I recalled coming home after attending a seminar on maximizing the efficiency of workspaces. The instructor stressed the importance of getting the components as close to the operator as possible to maximize efficiency and minimize the assembly time. Thinking I'd be doing Patty a favor by helping her with her efficiency in the kitchen, I began rearranging items in the cabinets. I was badly mistaken. She told me kindly but firmly, "You're not my supervisor. This is *my* kitchen."

I stroked Lucky's soft warm fur and massaged his ears. The warmth of his body in my lap took the chill off my legs. Periodically, his ears perked up suggesting he was hearing sounds my ears could not. I continued stoking his head and spoke to him in a gentle, reassuring tone.

"I'm glad you're here, Lucky. I've missed not having Sheba around. Do you think we'll be happy together? Yeah, I think so too."

A dreariness settled into my head much like a fog invading the shoreline of a lake. Sleep called out to me provocatively. Its spell splintered my thoughts into fragments. Closing my eyes would certainly usher in the most peaceful sleep, but I resisted.

The sound of rollers gliding across the sliding glass door track interrupted the quietness.

"Honey, the boys are asleep. I'm going to bed," Patty said softly.

"Okay, I'll be right in."

As the door closed, I recalled what I knew of Lucky's story. Marsha's son-in-law, a conservation officer, said he found him while on patrol in the remote fields of Upstate New York. As he neared the edge of the Barge Canal, he heard what sounded like a puppy yelping. The canal served as an inland waterway that cut across a good portion of our state, connecting Lake Ontario to the Hudson River. The waterway bypassed the long journey down the St. Lawrence River to the Atlantic Ocean. A century earlier the canal was bustling with barge traffic hauling grain and coal from Buffalo to New York

City and points in between. More recently it was used by an occasional recreational boater.

The conservation officer walked along the canal searching for the source of the distress. He eventually came upon a creature floating in the water paddling for his life. The officer took the puppy home after no one claimed him. It was Marsha's grandson who named him Lucky because he was *lucky* to be alive.

Sleep dogged me now. It was pointless to try to resist it. I gathered myself up and carried Lucky inside.

Heavy breathing escaped through the opening of Mike's room. I quietly opened the door of Lucky's pen and gently coaxed him inside. He willingly complied perhaps recalling all the fun he had earlier in the evening with Dan and Mike. A soft glow spilled into the room from a nightlight we kept plugged into an outlet in the hallway. It wasn't until I closed and latched the door that my new friend realized he was going to be left alone.

"Be a good dog, Lucky. Lie down and go to sleep."

The last thing I saw when I glanced over my shoulder was the whites of his eyes darting nervously back and forth.

I collapsed in the bed. Sleep came almost immediately after my head hit the pillow. I was oblivious to Lucky's soft whimper that rose out of the quietness. Unattended, it slowly grew in volume. Any noise my ears might have heard didn't register. The whimpers grew louder.

"Mom, make him stop," Mike said harshly.

Politeness is not a trait of anyone yanked out of a sound sleep and denied reentry.

"It will be okay, just ignore him," Patty answered.

Soft yaps accompanied the whimpers.

"M-o-m!"

"Bill," Patty said, shaking me, "go check on Lucky."

"He's okay," I muttered, clutching my pillow. "I just penned him up."

"No. You've been sleeping. He's been whining for almost an hour."

Lucky, hearing people's voices, responded with increased vigor. The yaps grew louder.

"M-o-m!"

"Your father is coming!"

I stumbled out of bed and felt my way along the walls to Mike's room. Without my glasses, I relied on my toes to probe the carpet in front of me, hoping to avoid any rogue Legos.

Lucky was standing in his pen, awaiting his release. His tail banged against the side of the pen like a tambourine. I stared at him unsure of what I should do. My drowsy state produced no immediate solution.

"How are you doing, Mike?"

"Dad, he won't stop whining."

"Lucky, you aren't making any friends tonight."

"He can't understand you, he's just a stupid dog."

"Be nice. He's in a strange place and he's probably lonely."

Lonely? Maybe that's the solution.

"Mike, what if I go get Lady and have her sleep in your room tonight?"

These words were music to Mike's ears. Dan currently had the sole privilege of sleeping with Lady. He won the latest round, selling Mike a line about needing Lady for protection because he slept alone in the basement.

I went to fetch Lady, aware my solution would likely be a one-night event. When Dan woke up in the morning and discovered someone had stolen the dog from his room, he wouldn't be happy.

Dan's bedroom door made a low creaking sound when I opened it.

"Lady, come here, girl."

She emerged from the darkened interior of the room and followed me up the stairs without protest. I released my secret weapon into Mike's room and prayed it would do the trick.

"Good night, Mike."

"'Night, Dad," he said, smiling as he clutched Lady.

Home

What constitutes a home? Is it a location, a feeling, or can it also be something more? Home for Lucky equated to an unobstructed run of the house (which he loved) and his dog crate (not so much). We penned him up whenever we left him home alone to prevent his destructive behavior from resurfacing. We later learned this behavior was due to separation anxiety most likely because he was abandoned as a puppy. We didn't pen him up to be cruel—rather, to create a safe and secure place for him.

For humans, home should also serve as a place of safety and comfort. Ideally, it would be an environment that fosters personal growth and healing, a place where needs are met. For many people, however, this is not the case; it's not their reality. Home, for them, is a place of brokenness, traumatic experiences, or worse. For them a "happy" home exists only in fairy tales.

It is easy to define home as a place. I had a lot of them during the first ten years I was married. Patty and I moved eight different times during that period. The first home I can remember as a five-year-old was a small ranch my parents bought in the suburbs. I lived there with my parents, four siblings, and a dog named Boots. Each day of my existence began and ended in that place. There I learned about love, Jesus, and the difference between right and wrong.

In college I shared a dorm room with a roommate, but I considered the entire campus my home. For the first time in my life, home was a place that did not include my parents. It was an odd feeling returning to my childhood home on a semester break. I felt more like a visitor than a resident. It was in college that I met my future wife and where we charted a new course together. She and I worked hard to merge both our childhood homes into a place we could call home.

Our joint home became a special place where Patty and I taught *our* children about love, Jesus, and the meaning of right and wrong. One day, in the future, our "nest" will be empty but full of material things that we've dragged along with us from place to place. In that future, we will likely have to downsize, move into smaller living quarters, and eliminate much of our material goods. As I continue to age, there will come a day when my faculties diminish. At that point the elements of what I once considered home will be slowly pried from my grasp, leaving me with a fading memory of what once was. Thankfully, a physical "home" does not lay an exclusive claim to the meaning of the word.

Outside the physical realm of our five senses lies a home that is spiritual in nature. One that engages the heart, mind, and soul in a realm that is eternal. Relationships with the significant people or creatures in our lives reach beyond the physical realm. These relationships foster deep emotions such as happiness, passion, anguish, and heartache. This would account for my deep feelings over the loss of Sheba. Those feelings lingered far longer than the loss of our first home.

When I consider the relationship I have with Patty, it doesn't matter where I am or what I'm doing just as long as I can spend time with her. When we were dating back in college, we wrote letters and mailed them to each other while we were apart. I vividly remember the desperate yearning in my heart when days passed and I didn't receive a letter or talk to her on the phone. Over the years, our minds, hearts and souls have become intertwined. My relationship with her is also my home.

As a young adult, I learned I could have a relationship with the living God of the Bible (Psalm 42:2). When I invited Jesus into my life, I gave him a home in my heart (Ephesians 3:17), and He gave me the promise of a heavenly home (John 14:1–4). Those who truly know Him long to stay connected to Him through prayer, meditation, and the Scriptures. Jesus, during His time on earth, called this the greatest commandment: "Love the Lord your God with all your heart and with all your soul and with all your mind" (Matthew 22:37). Our relationship with God is an eternal home.

Putting my relationship with God first helps me with all my other relationships (Matthew 6:33). Putting God in the center of everything changes everything (Romans 12:2). My old self-centered way of life no longer determines who I am (2 Corinthians 5:17).

Because He is *the* living God, I can walk with Him, talk to Him, and listen for His voice in the quietness of my heart. When I draw near to God, I learn about what pleases Him (Romans 14:17–18). We are promised that if we draw near to Him, He will draw near to us (James 4:8). By placing my trust in Him and acknowledging Him in everything I do, He will direct the path I'm traveling on for the rest of my life (Proverbs 3:5–6).

I am not alone in my pursuit of God; others are pursuing Him also. These are people I might not normally associate with but for our common interest in the pursuit of God. Pockets of people who believe in God form a community and gather in a place they call God's house. True community doesn't manipulate relationships for personal gain or make others feel unwelcome. Instead, believers genuinely strive to help, protect, and care for their Christian brothers and sisters (Ephesians 4:15–16). In this "home" people grow spiritually as they worship God and serve others in His name.

A church home is a forerunner of a believer's ultimate destination: heaven. Simply put, heaven is the culmination of everything we call home. More importantly, it's the place where God dwells. This is the prize believers long for and is the purpose behind their striving (Colossians 3:1–2). Entrance into this kingdom is granted solely on the basis on having established a relationship with God who made us in His own image and yearns to welcome us—home (2 Corinthians 5:1)!

One thing I ask from the LORD, this only do I seek: that I may dwell in the house of the LORD all the days of my life, to gaze on the beauty of the LORD and to seek him in his temple. (Psalm 27:4)

"Do not let your hearts be troubled. You believe in God; believe also in me [Jesus]. My Father's house has many rooms; if that were not so, would I have told you that I am going there to prepare a place for you?" (John 14:1–2)

I pray that from his glorious, unlimited resources he will empower you with inner strength through his Spirit. Then Christ will make his home in your hearts as you trust in him. Your roots will grow down into God's love and keep you strong. (Ephesians 3:16–17 NLT)

ELEVEN

Follow the Leader

I GOT UP EARLY the next morning and headed straight for Mike's room intending to take the dogs outside. I thought it odd that the door to Lucky's pen was standing open. *Where is he?* I approached Mike's bed thinking he was probably hiding under it. Mike was still zonked out; his blanket rose and fell with each heavy breath. *Two* heads suddenly shot up from among the pile of blankets as I approached. Lady acted pleased to see me while Lucky seemed a little unsure of what to do.

"Come," I said softly.

I offered a quiet whistle to exhort them on. Lady jumped down off the bed immediately. Lucky followed albeit tentatively. Both dogs trotted behind me down the hall to the kitchen. I treasured the quietness blanketing the house at this early hour. Passing the living room, I spotted the dim light of morning outlining the distant landscape with stray shafts of light here and there. The birds were already chirping like instrumentalists randomly tuning their instruments prior to the start of a symphony—a symphony that began the moment the sun broke the horizon.

It was an amusing sight watching Lucky fall in line behind Lady nose to tail like a trained circus elephant. When we reached the door, Lady hesitated just long enough for me to open it before sprinting out into the dark interior of the garage. A few seconds later the *thwap* of the plastic flap against the side of the house confirmed she had made her way outside. Lucky sat at my feet on the area rug, a vagabond unsure of what was expected of him.

"Go on. Go find Lady," I said, injecting enthusiasm into my voice.

Lucky just looked up at me and blinked. He wasn't going anywhere. I flicked on the garage light hoping it would inspire him to move. No response. I slowly pushed his butt with my foot toward the opening hoping to jump-start the process. He locked his front legs and dug his claws into the rug. No way was he venturing into the abyss. My effort amounted to little more than a carpet ride. I watched the rug crumple into a wad as it collided with the threshold.

Perhaps, if I lead by example, he'll follow.

I stepped out onto the garage floor and was immediately reminded of how quickly cold cement can suck the warmth out of bare feet.

"Lucky, come on!" I called with a sense of urgency.

Finally, he rose to his feet and gave his body a good shake. He was in no hurry, but I was. My feet were aching from the cold. Lucky hesitated again as if trying to remember why he rose to his feet. I grabbed him by the collar and quickly escorted him to the doggy door. I lifted the plastic flap so he could see Lady moving about outside. The neighbor's motion light had picked up Lady's movement and flooded the area with light. The frost-covered grass glistened in the artificial light. Lucky finally put two and two together and launched himself through the opening.

Satisfied with my effort, I hurried back inside and searched for my slippers. I rewarded myself by starting a pot of coffee. Several minutes passed before I heard Lady gently pawing at the kitchen door. Lucky trailed tightly behind her as she crossed the threshold and entered the warm confines of the kitchen.

Lady, no longer as spry as she used to be, wandered around the house looking for a place to lie down, which was usually a spot near one of the heat registers. I was curious what Lucky would do if I didn't offer him any direction. I leaned against the counter and sipped my coffee. Lucky followed Lady as she wandered around the house, paying close attention to her movements. This pattern, Lucky following Lady around, continued throughout the day. The manager inside me recognized what was happening. At the assembly plant, we used lead operators to mentor new employees to help them become certified. New employees learned more quickly when experienced operators worked alongside them.

Over the next several days, Lucky absorbed Lady's routine like a sponge. Wherever Lady went, he followed. If she barked at the UPS truck, he barked. Lucky observed and mimicked Lady's responses to my commands. This included watching me eat my cereal in the morning before I went to work. Lucky forced himself to wait patiently for a chance to lap up what little bit of the milk my spoon left behind. Lady didn't seem to mind sharing a couple of laps of milk. The relationship shared by the pair evolved into a communal existence.

Week one ended in dramatic fashion. Patty was working, so I busied myself in the kitchen emptying the dishwasher. Kit brushed up against my leg as he passed by. I thought nothing of it, mainly because I'm not extremely fond of cats unlike everyone else in the family. Lady and I tolerated Kit for the sake of family unity.

Make no mistake, Kit was a beautiful creature: a green-eyed, short-hair feline with a gorgeous smoky-gray coat. The problem with Kit was he seemed to know it. Whenever he waltzed into the living room, he was expecting someone to fawn over him. But on this particular evening the television offered more entertainment than any grand entrance he could make. *Star Trek: The Next Generation*, Dan and Mike's favorite program, was being beamed over the airwaves.

Lucky was relaxing in the corner of the room next to Lady when Kit entered. He did not understand why Lady was indifferent to Kit's entrance. The puppy inside Lucky couldn't ignore the creature standing in the center of the room purring loudly and twitching its tail. Up until that moment, Kit had done a masterful job steering clear of Lucky. Usually staying in his two main haunts, the outdoors and the basement, kept him out of harm's way.

Lucky had never been schooled in the traditions of majesty and pageantry. He had no understanding of what phrases such as "Look but don't touch" and "Keep your paws off the merchandise" meant. His heart was ruled by curiosity and instinct. So, when Lucky leaped on Kit, it caught our feline completely off guard. Kit's majesty hadn't been challenged in eons.

Stunned, Kit was unable to move under the weight of Lucky's front paws. Lucky began to familiarize himself with Kit, probing his underbelly and hind parts with his nose. Acting as though he had been violated, Kit hissed and spit but to no avail. Lacking no other recourse, Kit bit Lucky's paw and wriggled free.

Lucky didn't cower and retreat with his tail between his legs. His senses were enlivened. Instinct told him what to do next—give chase.

Kit made his first mistake by bolting for the sofa instead of heading for the basement. He leaped up on the back of the couch and paced back and forth on top of the cushions. Lucky couldn't restrain himself. The purring creature with the twitching tail was taunting him. Incredibly, Dan and Mike were still oblivious to what was going on. Their eyes were glued to the epic adventure unfolding before them.

Because we had recently purchased a new set of living room furniture, Kit was the only creature allowed on any of the pieces. It wasn't top-quality stuff, but we wanted to make it last. Kit and Lady both knew dogs weren't allowed on the furniture, but Lucky had yet to have it explained to him.

Lucky stormed the sofa and barked at Kit. A loud *meow* followed. It was at this moment that everyone in the house became aware of the situation. *This can't be good,* I thought. I abandoned my kitchen duties and dashed into the living room with my mind set on preventing bloodshed.

I arrived in time to see Lucky standing on the couch with Kit pinned under his front paws. Kit was about to make his second mistake: trying to climb the living room drapes without the benefit of claws on his front feet. Lady was on her feet trying to get a better view of the main event. She looked on like a wrestler waiting for her turn in a tag-team match.

Kit managed to wriggle free once everyone started shouting, "Bad dog." He made a desperate leap in the direction of the drapes, hoping to climb out of the range of Lucky's jaws. His body hit the windowpane with a thud before he crashed to the floor behind the sofa.

"Lucky, get down off the couch!" I yelled.

Dan and Mike continued to yell, "Bad dog!"

It was the first time Lucky had been yelled at since he'd been here. Frightened and unsure of what to do next, Lucky sprinted for the kitchen with his tail between his legs. Dan crawled behind the sofa and reemerged with Kit in his arms. Satisfied that no harm had come to Kit, I returned to the kitchen to check on Lucky. He sat on the area rug with his body pressed against the back door. His tail thumped against the floor when he saw me.

"What am I going to do with you, Lucky?"

He slowly made his way toward me slinking in a crouch. In that moment I realized I had two choices. I could push him away and continue to berate him, or I could bend down and offer him some love. I chose to offer him mercy. I wasn't looking for a creature to lord over; I was looking for a friend.

For the next several weeks we decided to let the animals sort things out for themselves. Lucky came to tolerate Kit but only after being bitten on the tip of his nose several times. Most of those incidents occurred because Lucky wanted Kit to play with him when the cat had no desire to do so. Lucky remained suspicious of Kit. Who knows, maybe he was looking for a chance to get even. Lucky and I now had something in common. Cats just weren't worth the trouble.

It didn't take me long to realize I was out of practice when it came to raising a puppy. Our home required constant housekeeping and bore the distinctive charm of a family raising a toddler. Dog toys, blankets, and an assortment of shredded objects littered the floor on any given day. Our children were preschoolers when we went through this phase with Lady. Back then we had an excuse if company showed up and our house was in shambles.

As with any toddler, the task of keeping Lucky occupied and out of mischief was a constant battle. Since I'd lobbied so hard to get him, I knew this responsibility ultimately fell on my shoulders. Thankfully, I didn't feel burdened by it. Patty would argue the reason it didn't bother me was because I spent most of my day at work. Perhaps she was right. Regardless, I was willing to expend the time needed to raise him if the outcome mirrored anything close to the bond I had with Sheba. Spending time with him seemed like the fastest way to make it happen.

Little by little, Lucky's personality began to emerge. Riding in the car proved to be my first exposure to it. Patty encouraged me to "take *him* along" whenever I left the house to run a quick errand. Her sweet voice would call my name when I least expected it.

"Bill, are you going out?"

"Yeah, I'm making a run to the store. Do you need anything?"

"Why don't you take Lucky with you?"

Lady, a poster child for peace and harmony at this stage of her life, was happy to stay home and guard the rest of the clan. Both she and Patty appreciated the quietness Lucky left behind in the wake of his departure.

I have little or no memory of taking Lady with me to run errands. She almost always stayed home. There were at least two reasons for this that I can think of. First, when the boys were little, I took *them* with me and left the dog behind. Two toddlers were a handful without bringing a dog along for the ride. Second, any trips we did make with Lady resulted in fur being shed all over the car. Her black fur seemed to blend in with the fabric on the car seats and would reattach itself to Patty and me whenever we sat on them in our dress clothes.

Fortunately, Lucky loved to accompany me on my errands. "Do you want to go for a ride?" quickly became part of his vocabulary. Whenever he heard the words, he'd race to the door, bark, and jump up and down until we made our exit. Coaxing him into a vehicle required no effort whatsoever, but keeping him seated once he got inside was always a challenge.

Lucky was always the first one in the vehicle, which meant he could choose any seat. He always chose the driver's seat. I added "move over" to his vocabulary.

Exiting the vehicle presented its own challenges. When the door opened, Lucky planned on being the first one out. It never occurred to him that maybe he was supposed to stay behind and await my return. I blocked his attempts to vault over me on more than one occasion, which usually resulted in me colliding with his bony head. Sometimes I came come home with scratches on my body when I was forced to wrestle him off me.

Our first rides together bordered on being hazardous. As I drove, Lucky felt compelled to duck under my arm and force it upward with his head to gain access to my lap. I didn't like losing my grip on the steering wheel unexpectedly. I was forced to drive with my elbow pointed outward to ward off his attempts to dive under or leap over my arm clutching the steering wheel. It took several outings before Lucky caught on that it was a bad thing to distract the driver. He insisted on compromise, so I permitted him to rest his head in my lap as I drove.

He never lost his affinity for the driver's seat, however. Whenever I left him in the vehicle, he immediately occupied my seat. People walking past our vehicle invariably did a double take when they spotted Lucky sitting in the driver's seat peering out over the steering wheel as he waited for my return.

Ultimately, the use of power windows ushered in a peaceful and much safer experience for both of us. Lucky could be coaxed into any seat in the vehicle simply by powering down the corresponding window. An open window offered a smorgasbord of scents, all of which seemed to have an intoxicating effect on him. He took the air in through his open mouth and appeared to taste it with his tongue. Once he got a mouthful, he gulped and licked his chops as his ears flapped in the breeze. Every ride was a cultural enrichment activity for him, even the routine trips to the local service station for gasoline.

~

Follow the Leader

Lucky learned quickly how things were done at our house because Lady mentored him, probably more than we realized. He followed Lady around the house because he lacked the necessary knowledge and experience. Following Lady around may have gotten him off to a good start, but until he followed the leader of the household and did the things I asked of him, he wasn't going to succeed.

When I was young, I acted in a similar manner. I learned to do things by having others mentor me. After following someone's lead, I gained experience and confidence and learned how to act in certain situations. But I still needed to follow whoever was leading me to be successful, whether that was my parents, a teacher, or a baseball coach.

My parents had a lot to do with my spiritual upbringing. They had me baptized as an infant and raised me in a Christian home. They carted us kids to church almost every Sunday without fail. I could not call myself a true Christian, however, until I knew Jesus personally and submitted myself to His leadership by placing my trust in Him.

To illustrate my point, consider your approach to the Lord's prayer. On any given Sunday thousands of people assemble in churches around the globe. Many of those people will likely recite the Lord's Prayer from memory like a poem as part of a litany. But

Jesus gave this prayer to His followers as a means to communicate directly to God.

Our Father in heaven, hallowed be your name, your kingdom come, your will be done, on earth as it is in heaven. Give us today our daily bread. Forgive us our debts, as we also have forgiven our debtors. And lead us not into temptation, but deliver us from the evil one (Matthew 6:9–13).

Do you and I recite this prayer simply to follow the leader of a worship service, or are we using it as a model to talk directly to God?

"Our Father." It's hard not to immediately begin making comparisons to my earthly father. I loved him above all men. The same may not hold true for those who had an unloving, abusive, or absentee father, however.

Jesus addressed God as His father, but He also chose the word *our* because true believers are children of God. God is *the* ultimate Father. He is not flawed like our earthly fathers. Our heavenly Father loves us unconditionally and will provide for all our needs. We can gain a better understanding of our heavenly Father by examining the life of Jesus. He told his followers, if they had had seen Him, they had seen his Father, God (John 14:8–9).

"In heaven." Heaven is a real place and not some idea dreamed up to help us cope with difficulties. Heaven's draw is the human ideal: immortality, vitality, and a life free from limitations, defects, and disease; a place of peace, prosperity, and rest. Yet if people don't know God personally, how much confidence can they have in their belief that they are heaven bound?

My limited understanding wants to define heaven with clear tight boundaries. But as I age, I've come to realize heaven is not confined to the atmosphere or the vast reaches of outer space; it has many dimensions and can exist in and around me. From His throne in heaven, God rules the entire universe. Nothing has dominion over Him. When we invite God into our hearts, our relationship with Him gets personal. Those who have a personal relationship with God will certainly join Him in heaven one day (John 14:1–3).

"Hallowed be your name." Translation: I hold God's name above all names, and with reverence I honor it. When I hallow God's name, I recognize His power and authority and affirm He is the absolute standard of truth and holiness. I also acknowledge He is God and I am not. As a Christian, I choose to allow God to purify my heart (Psalm 51:10).

"Your kingdom come." The Christian is taught that this world is not our home. We are pilgrims or transients just passing through. Some Christians, however, are doing so well at managing their finances and careers that they've lost focus. They've been building their own kingdoms here on earth. The imminent return of Christ to establish His Father's kingdom is something they hope will not interfere with their plans.

When a believer prays, "your kingdom come," I believe he or she is asking God for two things. First, in this present age, it's an invitation for God to occupy the throne of their heart. Second, the believer is asking God to establish His kingdom here on earth in the age to come for all eternity (Revelation 21:2–3). The Christian longs to be a citizen in a kingdom where truth and justice prevail.

"Your will be done." For a good part of my life I winced whenever I came to this phrase. To ask God to do His will in my life meant I had to surrender the fortress I constructed around my will. I worried He might ask me to do something I wouldn't be able to do. For the longest time there were areas of my life I refused to let go of. Eventually, I came to understand that by not surrendering my will I was being disobedient and sinning against God. As a Christian it's my responsibility to see that my will remains in harmony with His. When I deny God my will, I limit His ability to work in my life and rob myself of untold blessings (Psalm 40:8; Proverbs 10:6).

"On earth as it is in heaven." God accomplishes His will in heaven. In heaven there is no chaos or dissent. It's a place of harmony, peace, and joy. The folks who make it their home serve God willingly as evidenced by their unending, joyful adoration and praise.

It is quite a different picture here on earth where God's name is profaned with unsettling regularity. Some people profess to hate God while others refuse to believe He exists. We watch helplessly as our world embraces hate and violence instead of love and peace. Accomplishing God's will "on earth as it is in heaven" appears at times to be a losing proposition and beyond the scope of mortal men and women who love God.

However, by praying for God's will to be accomplished on earth, we are inviting God to work in our hearts and through our lives. We are inviting Him to use us to accomplish His will no matter how insignificant the task may be. There is coming a day when God will inhabit our broken planet and establish His kingdom here (Revelation 11:15).

"Give us today our daily bread." Up until this point, the Lord's Prayer has focused on matters of the soul and spirit. But God knows our every need, including our physical need for food. The inclusion of food in the prayer links our physical needs to our spiritual needs (John 6:33–35). Not only does God know our needs, but He is also able to meet them. By praying for bread daily, we affirm God's ability to care for and maintain the world He created. He is not an absentee landlord. When I ask for daily bread, I affirm my dependence on Him as my provider.

"Forgive us our debts." The NIV translation uses the word *debts*. Other Bible translations use words like trespasses, shortcomings, sins, wrongdoings, etc. No matter what the variation of the word used, it is important to realize we need to ask for forgiveness because trespasses act as a barrier that separates us from God. When we humbly confess our sins before God, He forgives us (1 John 1:9). As Christians we need to search our hearts continually for the presence of evil. The Bible reminds us, "Blessed are the pure in heart, for they will see God" (Matthew 5:8). I have reached a point in my walk of faith that I don't want anything to encumber my relationship with God. Even so, I acknowledge I will always be a sinner in need of forgiveness.

"As we also have forgiven our debtors." There have certainly been persons who have wronged me. The question is, am I harboring resentment, jealousy, or bitterness toward them? When I harbor such things, it infects my heart like a poison. Borrowing a line from the movie *Frozen*, "Let it go!"

If there is a person continuing to transgress me, I might not be able to change them, but I can change with God's help. Is choosing not to forgive someone worth limiting who I am as a person? Am I willing to allow them to rob me of the ability to love others? God forgave me while I was still sinning against Him (Romans 5:7–8). He invited me, a sinner, to spend eternity with Him. If God forgave me, shouldn't I be willing to forgive others?

"And lead us not into temptation." Temptation itself is not sin, but it can lead us into sin if we let it. By design, temptation is intended to be personal and specific. It entices a given individual's passions and desires. Unfortunately, the guardian of our passions and desires happens to be our selfish and often rebellious will. Temptations do not come from God, but He can allow them to occur (James 1:13–15). "Lead us not into temptation" is a plea, an admission, that I am weak and vulnerable in certain areas of my life when it comes to warding off temptation.

"But deliver us from the evil one." It is important to understand that Satan was once the most brilliant, beautiful, and powerful creature ever created. *Was.* He was given the greatest authority and prominence in all of heaven, yet that was not good enough for him. He wanted more. Pride corrupted him. He sought to become like God (Isaiah 14:12–14). He craved the worship of men who were created in the image and likeness of God. If Lucifer who was made perfect in every way by heaven's standards could succumb to evil, what makes us think we can fare better apart from God? Satan's future destiny is certain; an eternal darkness awaits him along with all those who choose to embrace evil (Revelation 20:10).

We, on the other hand, are headed for a glorious destiny if we remain committed to God. His Spirit will guide us and help us avoid falling victim to temptation if we will but listen to Him (1 Corinthians 10:13).

I am not Christian because I belong to a religious denomination and can recite the Lord's Prayer from memory. I am a Christian because I have a personal relationship with God and have chosen to follow Him.

Whoever serves me must follow me; and where I am, my servant also will be. My Father will honor the one who serves me. (John 12:26)

TWELVE

A Season of Firsts

AS THE WEATHER TURNED COLDER, the thought of keeping our high-energy dog cooped up inside bordered on unthinkable. He was wearing out his welcome. Debris continued to litter the floor, and sofa cushions were constantly knocked askew. Because of Lucky, Dan's and Mike's homework papers occasionally required tape repairs, and their book covers bore his bite marks. I found myself reattaching blades that had fallen off the vertical blinds on a regular basis. They fell like flower petals whenever Lucky chased Kit or when the UPS truck stopped in our vicinity. So much for counting on the sofa to protect the drapes.

Outside, our options were limited. Lady and Lucky's kennel occupied about two hundred square feet and was barely large enough to serve as their potty area, let alone a dog run. So, as an act of home preservation, we relied on outdoor walks regardless of the weather.

The street we lived on curved continuously around our housing development, forming the shape of a kidney. It was immediately evident that Lucky's previous owners had little or no success in trying to get him to walk on a leash. Lucky's idea of a walk equated to dragging whoever held the leash to wherever he wanted to go. I found no pleasure in having my arm yanked out of its socket as he pulled me down the road like a reindeer trying to lift Santa's sleigh off the ground. Any effort to restrain him resulted in choking and gagging noises as he fought back. Thankfully, few, if any, neighbors were usually outside to witness his antics.

On a handful of occasions, I tried to walk both dogs at the same time, believing Lucky could benefit from Lady's experience and model behavior. Let's just say the results were never positive. Lady, now aged, wanted to plod along at my side at a leisurely pace. Lucky rebelled against the status quo and bolted in random directions.

Lady didn't seem hurt or disappointed by being left behind. I think she enjoyed the peace and quiet without Lucky. Since our children were never interested in going for a walk with Lucky unless I made them, Lady had plenty of company in the cozy confines of the house.

Mailboxes lined both sides of our street, which meant it was impossible to avoid all of them. Traffic prevented me from walking down the center of the road. The cars we encountered on our walk belonged to my neighbors, and I didn't want to give them the impression that I thought I owned the road. The mailbox posts drew Lucky to them like a magnet. He was compelled to cover the scents left by other dogs with his own urine. A routinely awkward moment for me came when a homeowner materialized from his home just as Lucky was watering their mailbox. Looking on, I felt like an accessory to a crime. I offered the glaring neighbor a sheepish smile and a weak wave before encouraging Lucky to bolt from the scene.

Since walking Lucky required so much time and effort, I eventually had to call for reinforcements. This meant enlisting the help of my lovely family. Surely, they wouldn't mind enjoying the fresh air and exercise while I was sitting in my chair at work behind a desk. Protests followed each person's first attempt, however. It became clear that Lucky enjoyed this activity more than the rest of us. Walkers returned home weary, their spirits broken. But Lucky begged for more.

We developed the habit of keeping the dog leash draped over the banister in the entryway. It was readily available for the poor soul assigned to take Lucky out for a walk. From his perch atop the over-size ottoman in the living room (yes, we bent the rules for Lucky and allowed him to sit on that one piece of furniture), he kept a watchful eye on that leash. No one in the family dared brush up against it when they passed by. If Lucky saw the leash wiggle, even the slightest bit, he believed a walk was imminent. He'd spring from the ottoman and go into a frenzy, barking, leaping, and obstructing the person trying to make their exit.

For weeks our daily walks amounted to a battle of wills. Lucky pulled excessively against the leash, while I countered, firmly pulling him back with a chorus of "heel," "heel," "heel." One marvelous day, Lucky's leash produced a gentle sag, but only after I fought with him halfway around the housing development. It was then I discovered how blissful a second lap around the block could be once Lucky settled down.

Like a track and field competitor, I overcame one hurdle only to encounter another. The longer Lucky's walks lasted, the greater the likelihood I would need a plastic bag for his dog poop. You'd think I could remember to grab a plastic bag before leaving the house. But with the effort required to get my coat on, tether Lucky to the leash, and get him calmed down enough to safely exit the house, this over-sight occurred all too often. I gained a new prospective of the phrase "going the extra mile." Each time I forgot, I had to return home for a bag before revisiting the scene of the crime. Eventually, plastic bags lined both Patty's and my coat pockets.

The worsening weather began to impact our walks. The rain, snow, or cold never bothered Lucky, but it bothered us. I set off in search of a safe means of indoor fun. Lady proved that a tennis ball could be a "house friendly" toy. I even had her demonstrate this for Lucky. When it was his turn, he chased the bouncing ball and returned.

"Good boy, Lucky," I said gleefully.

Lucky was more interested in playing keep-away than parting with the ball. So my effort to acquire the ball was not going to be like taking candy from a baby. His head bobbed and weaved to keep me from grabbing it. Eventually, I stood up and sandwiched his torso between my legs. I steadied his head with one hand while I tried to pry the ball loose from his jaws with the other as I uttered the command, "Give."

"That wasn't so hard, was it, Lucky?"

While I was saying the words, Lucky lunged for the ball and closed his jaws on my fingers.

"Ouch! Bad dog!"

I shoved him away to assess my wounds. Despite the searing pain, no blood was spilled. I knew Lucky was not trying to be mean. He was just intensely preoccupied with the notion of possessing the ball. From then on, I decided for play to continue I would wait for Lucky to surrender the ball. While I waited, I grabbed a section of the newspaper. I did not intend to use it as a tool for chastisement but, rather, to feign my disinterest in the ball by pretending to read the paper. When Lucky was good and ready to surrender the ball, he jumped on the ottoman, walked all over my legs, and crashed into the newspaper stretched between my hands. I was surprised to see him drop the ball in my lap.

Our games of fetch didn't last long. I conceded the ball after a few tosses. To help him unwind, I thought letting him chew on a ball would relieve some pent-up anxiety. Equipped with his prize, he trotted off and carried it behind an end table. There he punished the ball for its rebellious behavior. He tortured it by pulling the cloth covering off with his teeth.

A coverless ball got slimy when he mouthed it. Invariably, the ball would squirt from his jaws and roll away, causing Lucky to give chase. Whenever he burst out from behind the end table, the lamp sitting on it would wobble and occasionally tip over. Life with Lucky meant putting up with dented lamp shades.

All too often the ball found its way under the sofa. When that happened, he'd dig frantically at the fabric. Fortunately, the sofa was upholstered with a Herculon fabric that could withstand a beating, which was the main reason we purchased it in the first place. I found myself tasked with reattaching the upholstery trim along the bottom of the sofa on a regular basis. Eventually, I solved the problem by placing two-by-fours under each piece of furniture, which prevented the ball from rolling underneath.

The deathblow for the bald tennis ball came when one of Lucky's eyeteeth pierced its rubbery skin. A prolonged period of quiet followed the slaying. I quickly learned when our ultra-active dog grew quiet for an extended period, I needed to investigate.

"Lucky, what are you up to?"

When he gave no response, I followed a trial of rubber pieces to his lair. I thought, *No harm, no foul,* until the next day someone stepped in a pool of chunky vomit.

I did love Lucky, even though his stock was trending downward in everyone else's eyes. Our family found him too rough, too rambunctious, or too needy for their taste. Lucky was family, however, and they tolerated him, hoping that one day he'd grow out of it.

We were about a week away from Christmas, and I hadn't put up our tree yet. It was still out in the garage leaning against a wall. While it wasn't unusual for me to put up our tree late, this year I deliberately procrastinated because of Lucky.

"When are you going to put the tree up?" Patty asked as we relaxed in the living room.

"I'm worried what Lucky might do to it," I answered.

"So, you bought a tree and you're not going to put it up?"

"Well, I just have this picture in my mind of Lucky chasing Kit up the tree and knocking the whole thing over."

"Don't you think we've put it off long enough?" she replied. "Why don't we put on some Christmas music tomorrow morning and just get it done?"

"What about the ceramic ornaments your mother made? Aren't you worried one of them might get broken?"

"If Lucky breaks one, I guess I'll have to kill him," she added in jest.

"You are in a rare mood tonight. Apparently, you're not worried about it."

Patty smiled.

"Bill, I have it under control. You just make sure Lucky doesn't play with a ball in the house for as long as the tree is up."

The next morning with the cheerful sounds of Christmas emanating from the stereo, I dragged our Scotch pine tree from the garage and fulfilled my annual responsibility. The pitch from the tree gave the living room a fresh pine scent. Lucky looked on, tipping his head from side to side as I worked. I'm sure he was wondering why I'd dragged a tree into the house.

Once the tree was securely in the stand and covered with every strand of lights I could find, my role was finished. Patty and I sat together and studied the evergreen bearing the light of Christmas. The dogs busied themselves sniffing the branches and pawing at the skirt we placed under the tree, convinced it was their new bed. After several rebukes, they gave up trying.

It was Patty's job to adorn the tree. Her most precious ornaments remained safely stowed in boxes. In their place she hung commercially available ornaments with a few unbreakable mementos sprinkled in. For Kit's benefit she hung a few cloth and plastic cat-friendly trinkets from the lower boughs.

Two evenings before Christmas, Kit waltzed into the living room as I sat with the boys watching a Christmas movie. Lucky rested on the ottoman, forcing my legs to the edge. Kit twitched his tail and purred loudly. Seeing he was being ignored, he wandered over to the tree to bat some of the ornaments with his paws. He passed right under Lucky's nose. If I didn't know better, I'd swear he did it deliberately. Lucky snapped to attention. His rigid body caught my attention. This was the moment I feared.

Kit lay down under the tree and began batting one of the gold-colored bulbs. Lucky launched himself from the ottoman.

"Lucky!" I yelled. "Bad dog. Leave the cat alone."

Of course, Lucky ignored me and headed straight for the cat. Thankfully, Kit didn't try to climb the tree. Instead, he dashed behind the couch. Lucky gave chase and brushed past the tree, dislodging a handful of ornaments as he passed.

"Bad dog," I said, rising to my feet. I pounded my feet on the floor for emphasis. Lucky broke off his assault and sprinted out of the living room heading for the back door in the kitchen. I did not follow him.

The next day I took all the presents we had wrapped and formed a retaining wall under the base of the tree to prevent the animals from loitering anywhere near it. I deemed the boys were old enough not to unwrap their presents before Christmas morning. What choice did I have? Of course, this didn't stop Dan and Mike from "inspecting" the gifts when we weren't looking.

When Christmas morning arrived, it was different from past Christmases because Dan and Mike decided to have a contest to see who could "sleep in" the longest. Patty and I were up and dressed and well into our preparations for a full breakfast before I caught on to what was happening. I declared their contest over and told them they had ten minutes to stumble out of bed and join us. Lucky and I ventured over to his Christmas stocking while we waited. Lucky didn't know this day was different from any other. I sat on the floor with my arms around him unwrapping the handful of gifts I'd gotten for him: a hard rubber ball with a bell inside, a chew bone, and a stuffed squeaky toy that would probably be on life support before the end of the day. It was Lucky's first Christmas and that was all that mattered.

~

Firsts

Lucky's first months with us proved to be both exciting and challenging. I recall looking on with excitement as he experienced many things for the first time. The puzzled look on his face when I dragged a live Christmas tree into the house was priceless. Out of these experiences and achievements a singularity emerged. He was becoming devoted to the one who met his needs and loved him. Many thoughts occurred to me as I reflected on the meaning of the word *first*.

What is it about the word that I find intriguing? For starters, first offers a person an alluring gateway to experience something they have never done before. Hence the phrase "a first time for everything." *Firsts* offers us a means of discovering new likes and dislikes. Doing something for the first time may reveal a previously unknown talent or giftedness.

I learned from my college days that *first* can mean a prerequisite or requirement that must be completed in a series of courses. In the game of baseball, a run is scored after you touch all the bases, starting with first base. When constructing an object, it is wise to consult the instructions first.

Perhaps the most desirable meaning of the word *first* occurs in the arena of achievement. What could be more satisfying than being recognized for besting those you competed against, even if the only person competing is you. A first-place achievement provides the victor with a platform to showcase their greatness. Achievements of this type usually require hard work and sacrifice. It is the idea of sacrifice that leads to the greatest meaning of the word *first*.

Establishing a priority elevates one activity, thing, or person above all others. The sum of too many competing priorities leads to mediocrity. When designated as *first*, a priority becomes the filter or lens through which one's existence is viewed and the basis on which they make their decisions.

We live in a culture that promotes putting *self* first. Self, then, becomes the lens through which life is viewed and a basis for decision making. For those adopting an "it's all about me" mentality, all aspects of their life become self-serving.

If a personal relationship were to develop in the life of a self-serving individual, *self* will stand in the way of enrichment. To have a significant relationship with someone, *self* must find a way to become less of a priority. If *self* can be surrendered and the other person given priority, the prospect of a deep and meaningful relationship becomes more likely and can be sustained.

Our shared experiences drew Lucky and me closer together. When I took him for a walk, his concern wasn't "where are you taking me?" He just wanted to be outside having fun with me. I found myself planning things that would make our activities together more meaningful. When I observed Lucky's dedication and devotion to me, it caused me to take stock of my own priorities. *What am I doing to prioritize the important people in my life, especially the God I profess to serve? Do I dare make God the "first" priority in my life and use my knowledge of Him as the basis on which I make decisions?*

Turning over authority or control of your life to someone else is a risky proposition. What if their goals differ from mine? What if I hate the direction the person wants to take me?

God is no ordinary companion, provider, leader, or guide (Psalm 119:105; Genesis 22:14). He knows us better than we know ourselves (Psalm 139:1–5). He understands what will make us truly happy (Psalm 37:4–5). We can be certain God's love for us will never fail (Psalm 57:10).

The most treasured prospect of all is that God can use us just as we are. The disappointments, hurts, or losses we've experienced, as well as any talents and interests we have, make us uniquely qualified individuals and his prized possessions (1 Corinthians 1:26–28).

Putting God first in my life does not leave me empty-handed. He knows *specifically* what I need and *exactly* when I need it (Matthew 6:33; John 6:35). He is Lord over the universe who loves to care for his own (Isaiah 46:4).

How committed am I to being in a relationship with God (Colossians 3:17)? Is He in my waking thoughts? Do I think of Him throughout the day and as sleep approaches in the evening (Psalm 1:1–2)? Are my words and actions guided by the thought of pleasing Him (Psalm 119:11)? As I journey through life, I need to be reminded that there is no status quo in my relationship with God. I must choose to put God first every day, lest the cares of this world steal my heart away from Him. (Matthew 6:24).

He [Jesus] asked them, "What were you arguing about on the road?"

But they [the disciples] kept quiet because on the way they had argued about who was the greatest. Sitting down, Jesus called the Twelve and said, "Anyone who wants to be first must be the very last, and the servant of all." (Mark 9:33–35)

Do you not know that in a race all the runners run, but only one gets the prize? Run in such a way as to get the prize. Everyone who competes in the games goes into strict training. They do it to get a crown that will not last, but we do it to get a crown that will last forever. (1 Corinthians 9:24–25)

But seek first his kingdom and his righteousness, and all these things will be given to you as well. (Matthew 6:33)

THIRTEEN

Abide with Me

January 1999

FESTIVE SNOWFALL and the Christmas music that accompanied it have always been a welcome introduction to the season. But real winter began in January when the weather turned colder and Jack Frost applied a chokehold with his icy grip. Straightening up the garage was my first task of the new year. I never looked forward to doing it. It wasn't because of the work involved; rather, it was being forced to concede that winter was going to be with us for a while.

The task was a relatively easy one. It involved clearing the floor of toys, bikes, and sporting goods equipment so that we could park both our vehicles inside. Scraping ice off my windshield on a daily basis was one of my least favorite jobs. My work wasn't finished until I made a clear path to the snowblower.

This year there was more gear to stow away than usual. "Santa" purchased rollerblades for every member of the family. The boys also acquired street hockey gear; elbow and knee pads, sticks, pucks, and goals made of PVC piping. While gathering up the items and stowing them in the giant bin that sat on the floor of our garage, I spotted a racquet and a canister of balls left over from my gym membership days.

Picking up the dusty racquet, I twirled it in my hand and immediately thought of Lucky. I removed one of the bright blue balls from the canister and was impressed by how lively it still was. The tennis balls Lucky and I played with in the living room had a rather wimpy bounce compared to these. I tapped the ball with the racquet and watched it spring to life. There was no doubt in my mind Lucky would freak out when he saw this ball bounce. It had thicker skin than a tennis ball, so it would probably tolerate his abuse.

Since Lucky and I were banned from playing with balls in the living room until all the Christmas decorations were put away, it seemed like the perfect opportunity to tempt him with the racquet-ball. The newly cleaned-out garage would make the perfect court to play on. I went inside to fetch my opponent.

As expected, Lucky saw the ball bounce once and needed no further persuading. He acted like I had just dangled a piece of raw meat under his nose. Based on his reaction, I was already anticipating the fun we were about to have. He followed me out into the garage bouncing up and down on all fours. I carefully protected the ball as Lucky repeatedly tried to grab the ball from me.

Standing in the center of the garage, I held out the orb and illustrated how I intended to strike it with the racket. Lucky immediately lunged for the hand I was holding the ball in. I whirled sideways just in time to protect my fingers from being raked by his teeth. I was determined to teach him to be patient. Unless he learned to wait, I'd accidentally strike him in the face with the racquet when we were playing.

"Lucky, no!" I yelled when he tried again to take the ball from me.

He sat there confused and stared at me, trying to figure out what I was doing. *Why is he showing me the ball if he doesn't want me to grab it?* I kept repeating the motion of me pretending to strike the ball until he stopped trying to lunge for it.

It caught him completely off guard when I smacked the ball.

He'd been lulled into complacency by my antics. Lagging a second behind the ball, Lucky rocketed toward the garage door but didn't get there in time. The ball caromed off the door, bounced once on the floor, and headed in my direction. I stepped aside and allowed it to whiz past me. It was time to get Lucky involved.

"Go get the ball," I said.

I really didn't need to say anything because Lucky was already after it. He pounced on the bright blue object, intending to subdue it permanently. When he squeezed it in his mouth, the ball squirted free. He ran it down as if he were chasing a live animal. *This is fun*, I thought as I watched him trot around the perimeter of the garage holding his head high while mouthing the ball. I let him have his victory lap.

Once he stopped moving, I grabbed hold of his collar and gave the "give" command several times while carefully trying to extract the ball from his jaws. Eventually, he yielded.

I returned to the center of the garage and struck the same pose Lucky had seen earlier. This time he waited. I struck the ball again, directing it toward the garage door. When the ball returned, I caught it rather than swatting it. I would be less likely to hurt Lucky if I caught the rebounds off the door instead of trying to hit them.

"Did you see that? That's how we're going to play," I said, knowing full well I was having a conversation with myself. "I'll hit the ball, and you try to grab it before I do."

I repeated this process a couple more times. Each time, Lucky failed to secure the ball. He wasn't getting discouraged; it had the reverse effect. I could see the intensity building in his eyes. When I saw the drool dripping from his mouth, I pitied the ball.

Lucky was ready for action when I struck the ball again. Because I aimed a little lower this time, he was able to block the rebound with his body and secure it in his mouth.

"Good dog! You just scored your first point. That makes the score one to zero," I joked.

Lucky could care less about the score. He had the ball. He was more interested in playing his own game—keep-away. The slimy ball squirted from his mouth in my direction. I snatched it out of the air and without hesitation swatted it in the direction of the garage door. I caught the ball when it returned.

"I'll take a point for that one," I said, laughing out loud.

As play continued, Lucky resorted to guarding me. He desperately wanted the ball. We had a little WrestleMania fun each time the ball headed for us. Each of us tried to keep the other one from grabbing the bouncing ball.

My next serve revealed the one obstacle neither of us had control over. Three-inch-high metal ribs ran along the length of the garage door. They were spaced about fifteen inches apart, which made my serves more challenging. If the ball hit any part of a rib, it caromed unpredictably: straight up, straight down, or in a high, arcing lob over my head. Virtually all the wild rebounds benefitted Lucky.

"The score is tied five to five."

The ribs on the garage door interfered with my next three serves. Lucky chased them all down. Play stopped each time he grabbed the ball while I waited for him to finish his victory lap. Then I had to persuade him to give me the ball.

"Okay, Lucky, that gives you eight points. If you keep running off with the ball, I'm going to have to penalize you two points for delay of game."

Lucky's ears moved back and forth when I talked. His brown eyes darted between my mouth and my hand holding the ball. He was not about to be caught off guard when I smacked it. His pink tongue hung out the side of his mouth and wiggled as he panted.

"How are you doing, Lucky?"

He responded by bouncing up and down. Clearly, he wanted play to continue. I watched in amazement as Lucky gained confidence with each volley. Once or twice, he launched himself in the air like a baseball player attempting to snag a fly ball as it flew past.

A feeling of triumph swept over me when our playtime ended. Lucky and I had created a memory, one that didn't involve the destruction of property. Our game gave us both some much-needed exercise.

"You win, but I want a rematch," I said, wrapping my arms around his neck and kissing him on the forehead.

Lucky watched me put the ball back in the canister. He wasn't happy about it, so I had to bribe him with a dog biscuit to coax him back into the house. It felt good to abide with him.

A few days later several inches of snow fell: the first significant snowfall of the winter. I looked out through the living room window that morning and marveled at the beauty of the landscape. It reminded me of a pound cake that had been doused with icing. Snow coated everything, including the dark gray branches of our maple trees. A few rebellious blades of grass managed to pierce the snowy blanket, giving the scene the appearance of sprinkles scattered over the frosty surface. The snow turned out to be the wet, sticky variety that would make a perfect snowman.

Caught up in the moment, I did something I hoped I wouldn't regret later. I opened the front door and let Lucky run loose in the yard. It was his first experience with a measurable amount of snow. Dan and Mike were already outside rolling the snow into spheres. Eventually, they would need a hand stacking the spheres on top of one another to make their snowman. I put on my winter gear and joined them. Lady stayed inside content to warm herself by the heat register.

Lucky sprinted across the yard like a crazed stallion. Miniature clouds of vapor leaked from his mouth as he sucked in cold air and expelled warm. His four webbed feet compressed the wet snow into clods, which flicked off his feet when he galloped. Every so often he'd lower his mouth to the ground and scoop up some of the snow to cool his tongue while he raced. A tiny white beard dripped from his snout each time he scooped more snow. Our wintry activity was just the sort of scene Charles Wysocki or Norman Rockwell would enjoy painting.

Lucky continued to release energy when he came inside. Sprinting from room to room with what we called the puppy crazies, he released the remaining clods of snow and dirt trapped in the webbing of his feet all over the house. I trailed behind him on cleanup duty.

The weather turned much colder in February, and lots of snow came with it. Cleaning out the driveway with a snowblower became an almost daily chore. I didn't mind running the snowblower, but I struggled with what to do with Lucky while I labored. When I left him inside, he got tangled up in the vertical blinds in the living room. He paced nervously back and forth, watching me clean out the driveway. I didn't want him outside with me because I knew he'd get in the way of the snowblower. Putting him out in the dog kennel ended up being the best option. From there, Lucky could study my movements from the landing I built for the dogs to help them enter and exit the doggy door.

I worked the snowblower up and down the driveway one day, trying to come up with some activity that could occupy Lucky during the winter months. I was getting tired of playing racquetball in an unheated garage donned in all my winter gear. After several close calls in the living room, we were one broken lamp away from balls being outright banned indoors. It shouldn't be that hard to find something to do outdoors. The winter weather didn't seem to bother Lucky. I resolved to visit the storage bin in the garage once I finished the driveway.

After putting the snowblower away, I let Lucky back in the garage. He snapped to attention when I handled the racquet and canister of balls. He had to wonder why I set them aside.

"There must be something in here I can use," I mused.

A smile stretched across my face when I spotted Dan's street hockey stick. I tapped the stick on the floor. I found the ball the boys used and dropped it on the floor. It had almost no bounce whatsoever. I took a playful swipe at it with the hockey stick just as Lucky was pouncing on it, and I smacked him in the face. On second thought this wouldn't do.

Lucky wove in between the cars mouthing the street hockey ball while I continued rummaging through the bin. I set aside an old baseball glove and several other items that were not suitable for the cold weather before spotting a Frisbee near the bottom of the bin. A smile crossed my face as memories of the fun I'd had with Sheba washed over me. I freed the disc from its confinement.

"Lucky, what's this?" I said, waving the faded red saucer.

Curious, Lucky trotted over to me and dropped the ball. I tapped him on the nose with the Frisbee a couple of times, which really annoyed him. He clamped down on it with jaws like an alligator when I did it again. He shook his head back and forth maintaining a vise grip on the Frisbee.

"Let go, Lucky," I said resolutely. "Give it to me!"

Lucky followed me over to the garage door opening. I had no doubt he would chase it because he had yet to take his eyes off it. I gave it a light toss and watched it land halfway down the driveway. It skidded along the frozen asphalt like a hockey puck before coming to a stop.

Lucky raced down the driveway and leaped on the lifeless Frisbee. After several attempts to pick it up, he raised his head and looked back at me. He moved the object around with his nose and continued making attempts to pick it up, but he couldn't. I roared with laughter. It wasn't until he pushed the disc into the snowbank and it flipped over that he was able to scoop up.

"Come, Lucky. Come," I called.

He held the Frisbee proudly in the air and trotted back to me. I gave him a good rubbing all over when he returned. Imagine my surprise when he dropped the flying disc at my feet and looked up at me. Lucky never voluntarily let go of anything. Did he know he needed me to make the disc fly?

I released the disc a second time, and Lucky streaked down the driveway after it. A crosswind caught the Frisbee and pushed it higher in the air before changing its flight path. The disc banked left and headed out into the side yard where it crash-landed. Lucky clawed his way over the snowbank bordering the driveway and slogged through the chest high snow. The half-buried Frisbee showered Lucky's face with snow when he attempted to pull it free. He stepped back and shook the snow from his face before attempting to grab it again. It was such a delight to laugh at his antics.

"Lucky, come," I yelled over the howling wind.

Lucky scampered back up the driveway with the Frisbee dangling from his mouth. I made no attempt to take it from him. I was just happy he abided by my command to come back. He had a mind of his own, and I knew I was rolling the dice every time I let him loose outside.

"Do you want me to throw it again?" I said, reaching down and patting his ribs.

Lucky bent low, straddling the object with his front paws. He licked his chops and steeled his eyes on it. If I hadn't been wearing gloves, I wouldn't have attempted to pick up the Frisbee without distracting him first. It was quite a painful experience when Lucky's teeth raked my fingers. Lucky bounced up and down and barked when I waved the Frisbee above his head.

"Frisbee," I said. "Fris-bee." I kept repeating the word as I waved it around.

Lucky was in motion, streaking down the driveway before the disc departed from my hand. He pounced on the whirling object before it skidded to a stop in the driveway. Lucky nosed it around again, trying to remember how he'd picked it up the last time. It looked like I found the entertainment I was searching for.

"You're a good dog!" I said when he returned.

Playing with the frisbee vaulted to the top of the list of games we played. For the time being it became part of my routine whenever I cleaned out the driveway with the snowblower. When we finished playing, I would toss the flying saucer into the storage bin. Each time I did this, Lucky stared at the bin not wanting to leave the Frisbee behind. He acted like he had unfinished business with it.

The remaining months of winter passed slowly. Lucky and I found time several days each week for him to fetch the Frisbee. His skill at chasing down the Frisbee improved significantly as the snow began to melt. He became so familiar with the word *Frisbee* that Patty and I had to resort to spelling it if we wanted to use it in conversation. If we accidentally said the word, we were faced with trying to calm down a crazed lunatic.

The great thing about playing Frisbee was we could do it in any weather. All I had to do was produce the disc, step back, and watch Lucky freak out. I decided to move our game into the backyard after Patty questioned why I wasn't more worried about him running off on me. She had a good point. The backyard would be safer, and Lucky would be less likely to be distracted by people walking by and vehicles using the street. The more times we played, the more certain I was he could catch the Frisbee midflight were it not for the snow impeding his progress. I couldn't wait for warmer weather to test his limits.

As spring approached, our method of letting the dogs out into the garage and relying on them to find their own way outside into the kennel came back to bite me. Lucky took it upon himself to grab the Frisbee out of the bin and carry it outside with him. Distracted by other matters, I forgot about the dogs. When Lady scratched at the door and came inside, Lucky was not with her. I decided I'd better go out and check up on him. I found him stretched out on the landing gnawing away at the Frisbee. I wasn't going to scold him for a few bite marks. But Lucky had chewed off an entire section of the outer rim, rendering it useless. Because Lucky failed to abide by my wishes, playing Frisbee had to be put on hold for several days until I could buy another one.

∾

Abide

As I contemplated the word *abide*, I learned that it's a verb that requires action. Its meaning can vary by the words connected to it. I considered three meanings of the word when I examined my relationship with Lucky: *abide with* me, *abide by* my commands, and *abide in* my love.

Lucky loved to play with me. Because of the time we spent

together, a bond formed between us. Despite his reckless tendencies, I loved to *abide with* him as much as he did with me.

The more time we spent together, the more I began to trust him. My trust granted him a measure of freedom. The freedom he enjoyed hinged on *abiding by* the commands I gave him. I expected him to "come" when I called. I expected him to "stay" when I told him to. If I said "give," I wasn't intending to punish him or deny him something he possessed. Lucky needed to trust my judgment on certain matters, which most of the time was an effort to preserve the integrity of the object we were playing with. Left alone with an object of his desire, he invariably rendered it useless.

In the long run, I hoped Lucky would learn to *abide in* my love just as Sheba had done. I wanted Lucky to understand who I was and what I stood for. Even if I wasn't present, I was counting on him knowing what I expected of him. I wanted the love I had for him to displace the separation anxiety he harbored.

Human relationships work the same way. *Abiding with* someone describes individuals who enjoy the connection they have with each other. They spend time together, sharing beliefs, goals, hobbies, and experiences. It's a phrase of endearment.

When someone asks you to *abide by* their wishes, there is an expectation you will comply. We are more likely to abide by a set of rules or instructions if we trust the one giving us direction. When we rebel, it probably has something to do with challenging that person's knowledge of a given situation or their authority over us. In my youth, if I went ahead and did something after I was told not to, negative consequences followed. Trusting the person and *abiding by* their wishes can lead to a deeper and more meaningful relationship.

If you enjoy *abiding with* someone and *abide by* their philosophy of living, you knowingly, or unknowingly, become more like them. On many occasions my mother used to say to me, "You're just like your father," regarding something I did or said. My father had made such an impression on me that he *abided in* me.

In a biblical context, Jesus asked His followers to "abide in him" (John 15:4). The connection He wanted to establish was a spiritual one. Jesus communicated to them that He was the way, the truth, and a new way of living (John 14:6).

When I chose to *abide in* Jesus, I moved past my familiarity with him. I didn't view the truth presented in the Bible as irrelevant, outdated, or meant to deprive me of my happiness. Instead, I had a desire to incorporate all I learned about Jesus into my way of living. By abiding in him, I became a follower (John 15:6–7). As I became more like Jesus, I hoped others would see the light I carried inside me (John 12:46).

The King James Version of the Bible uses the word *abide* seventy-seven times. John, one of Jesus's original twelve disciples, used it more than any other New Testament writer. A more modern rendering of *abiding in* Jesus can be accomplished by using the word *remain*.

Remain [abide] in me, as I also remain in you. . . . If you remain in me and I in you, you will bear much fruit; apart from me you can do nothing. If you do not remain in me, you are like a branch that is thrown away and withers; such branches are picked up, thrown into the fire and burned. If you remain in me and my words remain in you, ask whatever you wish, and it will be done for you. (John 15:4–7)

As for you, see that what you have heard from the beginning remains in you. If it does, you also will remain in the Son and in the Father. And this is what he promised us—eternal life. (1 John 2:24–25)

FOURTEEN

The Big Lie

THE DAYS of our two-dog family passed like condensation being wiped off a cold window. A new day formed over the previous one. The participants and routine remained the same, causing time to slip by unnoticed. Months passed, totaling a year.

In March winter began to falter. The sun's higher arc across the sky signaled the end of winter's reign. The once-mighty snowbanks lining the edges of our driveway rapidly melted away. Grass, matted under the weight of the snow, showed signs of springing back to life. Flower bulbs sprouted in the landscaped areas around our yard. Spring was just around the corner.

Lucky finished his second winter with us. He now displayed his full stature, moving shoulder to shoulder with Lady about the house. He weighed more than sixty pounds. The muscles in his legs, neck, and shoulders were fully developed. His bark grew in volume and deepened to the point that it startled bystanders.

As parents, we could also see time advancing in the lives of our children. Dan had entered high school, Mike, junior high. It was a mixed blessing watching our boys grow into young men. We knew the day would come when they'd declare their independence from us, but letting go of them a little piece at a time proved difficult.

Distracted by life's new opportunities, Dan and Mike spent less time with our dogs. This proved to be bad news for two devoted creatures counting on their continued love and affection. In the boy's absence, I attempted to bridge the gap.

Normally, the arrival of spring was something to be celebrated. But something was amiss in our house. Lady had lost her energy. She found it more difficult to rise with each passing day. She opted out of standing beside the boys as they waited for the school bus in our entryway. She whined and limped around the house, catching the attention of Lucky who renewed his practice of trailing behind her wherever she went. The fur on Lady's hindquarters became wet and matted. At first, I thought this was due to her incessant licking, but a faint smell of urine clung to her coat. When large wet spots began appearing on the floor underneath her, I knew it was time to pay the vet a visit. He confirmed we were nearing the end of her life that had spanned eleven years. I brought her back home, and together with the rest of the family we tried to make her as comfortable as possible.

For Dan and Mike, a relationship they had taken for granted was suddenly called into question. They struggled with the thought of an unbreakable bond being broken. Their comfortable world, which revolved around friends and school activities, was being turned upside down.

I wondered how meaningful Lady's remaining days would be now that so few remained. The boys returned to her side, hoping to capture a memory or two before the end came. My heart was ladened with sadness for Lady and our boys. I knew it would not be until she left us that the full weight of their grief would be felt.

Lady drank in the attention, content with her good fortune to have been loved, not by one but two devoted boys. When she could no longer rise on her own and had to be carried outside to go to the bathroom, I knew her time had come. Our fear of losing her shouldn't outweigh her suffering. Once the boys were at school, I called our veterinarian and made the necessary arrangements. Lucky followed me around the house as if he knew something out of the ordinary was about to happen.

I lifted Lady gently into my arms and watched as Lucky stood on his hind legs and delicately sniffed her muzzle. Lady reciprocated the gesture by licking his nose, a simple but profound good-bye. I carried Lady out to the car and laid her gently on a blanket. Cherished memories mingled with tears filled my eyes and clouded my vision as I drove to the vet. She deserved a better fate than the one being arranged for her.

I carried her into the vet's office wrapped in a blanket and held her in my lap. She whimpered softly, which deepened the ache settling in my chest. I was pretty sure she knew why we were here.

"It's okay, girl," I said, trying to convince myself to be brave.

As I waited for our appointed time, I thought about her life. Everything I had asked of Lady she had done, willingly and lovingly. She fulfilled her purpose. Our two boys grew up with a puppy to love, and they would never forget it. She patiently put up with being mauled by them when they were preschoolers and allowed herself to be confined in homemade forts. I chuckled at the thought of the ridiculous outfits the boys made her wear. Lady was always there for them—more than their working father ever could be.

I kissed her face and gently hugged her failing body. She offered a weak lick, but her kiss missed the mark. Life appeared to be draining from her body. A feeling of helplessness wrapped its tendrils around my heart, making it harder to breathe. When the time came to hand Lady over to a technician, it was difficult to see through my tears. A moment later, she was gone.

Lady's suffering had ended. She was freed from the constraints of her deteriorating physical body. I believed she was now in a better place. I was comforted by the thought of her running free over a field studded with flowers in the bright sunlight. The God who created dogs and loved them would not allow their spirits to roam in an abyss. Lady was in heaven, and I knew I'd be reunited with her someday. Cherished memories of her life continued to pass through my mind as I drove home alone.

Even though they had the time to say goodbye, Dan and Mike still took Lady's passing hard. It seemed unfair to them that their childhood best friend could be cruelly yanked from their grasp. Mercifully, Lady's death came in the middle of a busy school year. In kind fashion, friends and the activities they were involved in forced the passage of time, which served to dull their pain.

All eyes turned to Lucky to step in and fill the void left by Lady's passing. She had set the bar extremely high, however. How do you compete with the memory of a creature who could thrive in any situation they were placed in? Given Lucky's track record of being difficult to deal with, I was not prepared to say how long the increased affection would last. Nevertheless, I found it comforting to have Lucky with us during this time of loss.

~

The Big Lie

I heard a sermon regarding the restoration of all things. It resonated with my spirit because we had recently lost Lady. Our pastor, Wally Fleming said, "We were taught growing up that death was just part of the natural order of things." In other words, death is something we should accept as if it were part of God's plan from the beginning; you're born, you live for a time, and you die. Pastor Wally went on to say, "This is the biggest lie we've ever been told." God never intended death to be part of His creation. He is the God of the living, not the dead (Luke 20:38). I will carry these words with me for the rest of my days.

From experience I know, when a loved one dies, those of us who remain experience a significant amount of heartache and pain accompanied by an overwhelming feeling of loss. The physical connection we have with a departed loved one has been severed. We can no longer see, touch, smell, or hear them. Our physical separation from those we love produces a pain deep within us on a spiritual level. My family would have to cope with Lady's passing for a long time.

When we mourn the loss of a loved one, it's a reminder that all is not right with the world. Something is broken. Death was never meant to be the end of things. The spirit of life that resided in Lady had to go somewhere after it was released from her body. Is it wrong to believe that God, who created dogs and instilled a spirit of life in them, would in his absolute goodness call their spirits back to Himself? Would God in His infinite wisdom honor a creature who brought such joy to the people they served on earth? My answer is yes, I believe He would.

Human beings were created in the image and likeness of God (Genesis 1:27; 2:7). We are intended to be eternal beings like Him. The breath of life breathed into God's creatures was never intended to be extinguished. It was in the third chapter of Genesis that the disobedience of man brought the curse of death on every living creature (Genesis 3:19).

But physical death is not the end as many would have us believe. I believe that when we die, our spirit is freed from our physical body and continues its existence. It is our spirit that gives us our physical body its face and bodily features (Job 19:25–27). Our identity lies with our spirit, not in the tent we call our body (2 Corinthians 5:1–4).

The big question everyone should be asking is *where* their spirit will reside after their life ends. Will they live with God in heaven or by their own choosing live apart from him forever? The price has already been paid for our admission into heaven. This happened when Jesus died on the cross in our place. Salvation was, and still is, a free gift. Life boils down to a choice: accept the gift or reject it.

Jesus's resurrection from the dead offers proof that eternal life awaits those who believe in Him (Revelation 21:4–5). Eternal life, however, begins the moment we experience salvation. It's ours to enjoy now, even while we are still confined to our physical bodies. Why not put the limited amount of time we do have to good use by investing it in the people and creatures God has placed in our path.

Jesus said to her [Martha], "I am the resurrection and the life. The one who believes in me will live, even though they die; and whoever lives by believing in me will never die. Do you believe this?" "Yes,

Lord," she replied, "I believe that you are the Messiah, the Son of God, who is to come into the world." (John 11:25–27)

We were therefore buried with him through baptism into death in order that, just as Christ was raised from the dead through the glory of the Father, we too may live a new life. (Romans 6:4)

FIFTEEN

A New Normal

HOW DO you journey on when the dog you've known for a decade is gone? Do you draw strength from their memory, or do you cling to the dog who remains, drawing them closer and holding them tighter? A new normal lay before us as our family tried to cope with Lady's death.

I loved Lucky, but I had my doubts about him filling the void left in my heart. Earlier in his life, I thought he had the potential to become a "heart dog," the soul mate I dreamed of having. But with Lady's departure, I underestimated the positive effect she had on Lucky's behavior. When she was with us, Lucky made some positive strides.

The positive changes I saw in Lucky caused me to grow lax on penning him up when we left him alone in the house. I assumed he had forsaken the ghost of his past. Without Lady to keep him company, however, his separation anxiety returned. Our house became the battlefield where Lucky wrestled with it.

I was willing to overlook a mistake or two, but the mistakes were endless. Lucky kept us guessing as to when the next one would occur. A telltale sign soon emerged. All was well if Lucky greeted us excitedly at the door when we returned home. However, if he shied away from me, I took it upon myself to do a quick tour of the house. Invariably, my inspection brought to light a mess in some area of the house.

The "incidents" included chewing on things that didn't belong to him, tipping over garbage cans in the kitchen and bathroom. But the trouble didn't end there. He pulled the garbage out of the cans and littered the house with it. Sometimes there were pools of vomit on the floor when the ingested items he'd taken from the garbage disagreed with him. Other times he resorted to marking a chair leg in the kitchen with urine.

The proverbial last straw came when Patty baked a batch of two dozen chocolate chip cookies. Because we were pressed for time, she left them out on the kitchen table to cool as we hurried off to church.

"Bill, what happened to the cookies that were right here on the table?"

"I thought you took care of them."

"You don't think Lucky . . . ," she said, stopping midsentence.

"How could he? The paper bags are still on the table."

"Well, unless somebody broke into the house and stole the cookies, it had to be him."

"Where is he, by the way?" I asked.

It remained a mystery how Lucky could have taken the cookies off the paper bags without disturbing them. There wasn't a crumb left behind. Lucky usually left a trail of clues whenever he committed a crime. A couple days later I ventured out into the dog kennel to give it a cleaning. There I found "piles" of evidence of the theft left behind by Lucky after the cookies had passed through his system.

Lucky knew these types of behaviors wouldn't be tolerated. Yet he continually violated our trust. He knew even before I yelled, "Bad dog," that he was in trouble. I watched him sneak off in a low crouch with his tail tucked between his legs the moment I spotted the trouble. Each time, he retreated to the area rug in the kitchen by the back door. When I caught up with him, he couldn't bring himself to look in my direction. It was the most amusing sight to see his head locked sideways, refusing to look at me the whole time I talked to him. Had I not been so disappointed with his behavior, I would have found his antics hilarious.

To ease everyone's frustration, and to preserve our home, we resumed penning Lucky up whenever he was left alone. I didn't do it to punish him. I did it because I cared about him and wanted him to succeed. Of course, Lucky hated the idea. But I was willing to trade one step backward if it would gain us two steps forward. Each time I set him free, I welcomed him excitedly like a prodigal. I tried to ignore what was past and focus on the present.

Lucky constantly watched me whenever I was home. He followed me everywhere I went, from room to room. It was as if he was hoping I was about to do something that would involve him. Slowly but surely, he began walking in the present and avoiding the pitfalls of his past.

When spring weather warmed, it fostered the feeling that order had been restored to the universe. Activities intended for the outdoors could be resumed. Outside, I could play with Lucky as aggressively as I wanted to and not worry about breaking anything.

"Lucky," I whispered as he dozed on the ottoman.

I watched his ears wiggle.

"Where's your Frisbee?"

Lucky's head shot up. He whirled his head in my direction, believing he had just heard the most special word in all the universe. Had he dreamed it?

"Fris-bee," I articulated.

No, his ears had not deceived him. He sprang from the hassock like someone had stuck him with a pin and launched himself in my direction. I was lying on the couch across the room from him, which gave me just enough time to cover my face before Lucky started pawing at me. His thick tail thumped against the side of the sofa. I peeked through my crossed arms and spotted Lucky's gaze boring into me. He'd quit buying into my playful attempts to ignore him long ago.

Without warning I sprang to my feet and hit the floor on a dead run. I raced through the kitchen and out into the garage. Even with the element of surprise Lucky beat me to the bin where we now kept a small collection of Frisbees.

"What do you want?" I said, trying not to laugh as I snatched up a Frisbee.

Lucky bounced up and down. He knew what was coming and could hardly contain himself.

"Come on," I said, opening the back door of the garage.

I made my way out onto the deck. Lucky sprinted down the stairs ahead of me, waiting for me to join him in the backyard. I chuckled to myself wondering what Lucky would do if a burglar entered the house carrying a Frisbee.

Without the snow to slow him down, Lucky had perfected the art of plucking a Frisbee out of midair. On the bare ground, he could outrun any Frisbee I tossed. For me, it was the most pleasurable way to exercise Lucky, and one that caused me the least amount of pain. It helped that chasing the Frisbee was his favorite activity as well. He was a born leaper and very good at catching things in his mouth. Lucky carried less weight than Sheba and was probably faster. I characterized his movement as a blend of power and speed. It was truly a thing of beauty to witness.

The backyard where Lucky and I played presented several challenges. My main concern was the size of our playing field. It was a lot smaller than I would have liked. Our house was situated on the inside of a gradual curve in the street. Our lot, about one-third of an acre, resembled a slice of pie with a bite taken out of the point.

Both edges of the backyard were lined with evergreens: arborvitaes on one side, Canadian hemlock on the other. The width of our playground narrowed to about fifty feet where it abruptly ended at a third neighbor's stockade fence. This left us with less than a hundred feet of distance to work.

The disc escaped my hand in a low trajectory, like an arrow headed for its target. Lucky jetted after it in an all-out sprint. With the object just out of reach above his head, Lucky had precious few seconds to capture it. If he was unable to intervene, the Frisbee would hit the fence and fall lifeless to the ground. With the stride of a thoroughbred horse, Lucky outpaced the Frisbee, grabbing it delicately with his teeth with a second or two to spare. He immediately cut sharply to his left to avoid colliding with the fence.

My throws weren't soft tosses like a father teaching a young child how to play catch. Lucky wanted the Frisbee to travel fast, so that's what I gave him. This explains why an occasional toss cleared my neighbor's fence and landed in his backyard.

Mike was one of the nicest neighbors a homeowner could ask for. But I feared his German shepherd, Shelby. That dog snarled and barked at me whenever I approached the fence. I declined Mike's invitation to let myself into his backyard to fetch my errant throws because I didn't want to have a run-in with Shelby. Mike was kind enough to toss our Frisbee back over the fence whenever he noticed it in his yard.

Lucky easily handled tosses that climbed in altitude rather than flying in a flat trajectory. Because of his speed, he reached the object quickly and waited for it to fall out of the sky. He knew just when to leap and could pluck it out of the sky like a basketball player leaving his feet for a rebound. If for some reason his timing was off and he tipped the Frisbee, he prided himself on snatching it before it hit the ground.

On windy days when the Frisbee deviated from its flight path, Lucky thrived on the added degree of difficulty. A flying saucer that wildly changed its altitude or direction taunted Lucky. He vigorously chased those down with reckless abandon.

Lucky struggled with the concept of letting go of the Frisbee once he returned it to me. I could lift all sixty pounds of him off the ground without him parting with it. He seemed to be more possessive of the disc than I remember Sheba being.

Whether it was walking, playing Frisbee, or sharing the ottoman with him, this was the life Lucky offered. It was so different than life with Lady. She lived her adult life quietly behind the scenes. She rarely gave us any trouble. Was I naive to believe that Lucky would someday turn out the same? I often wondered why I put up with Lucky's shenanigans. Maybe his big brown eyes that took an interest in my every movement had something to do with it.

I wasn't the only one trying to figure out what to do with Lucky. One day I came home from work and found him snuggling up next to Patty.

"I thought Lucky wasn't supposed to be on the couch," I said, believing I had caught her breaking her own rule.

"He's not. See, his back feet are still on the floor."

"But what about the rest of him?"

"Lucky thinks he's following the rules," Patty answered with a wink.

This was life with Lucky, our new normal.

∼

A New Normal

Patty and I refer to any drastic change in our lifestyle as a "new normal." It's a reference we use to cope with a permanent setback or a hurdle that someone needs to overcome. Invariably, the setback involves a loss or restriction of some kind. We lived with a new normal following the loss of Lady. Other examples could involve avoiding salt in your diet or carrying an oxygen generator with you wherever you go. For many, a new normal results in the loss of personal freedom.

Life is full of experiences that require us to permanently change course. Consider what the prophet Jeremiah said in response to such a situation:

. . .

So I say, "My splendor is gone and all that I have hoped from the
LORD." I remember my affliction and my wandering, the bitterness
and the gall. I well remember them, and my soul is downcast within
me. Yet this I call to mind and therefore I have hope: Because of the
LORD's great love we are not consumed, for his compassions never
fail. They are new every morning; great is your faithfulness. I say to
myself, "The LORD is my portion; therefore I will wait for him." The
LORD is good to those whose hope is in him, to the one who seeks
him. (Lamentations 3:18–25)

A new normal doesn't only apply to negative situations, however.
For a follower of Jesus, it holds a positive meaning. It corresponds to
a new way of living found in the person of Jesus Christ. Jesus
describes the experience as being born again, where we can enjoy a
life free from the burdens of the past. In the eyes of God, once we've
been forgiven of our sins, those deeds are remembered no more
(Psalm 103:11–12). With this new lifestyle, children of God have the
assurance that they are truly loved (John 16:27) and that their life
matters to God. This life-giving freedom comes with the assurance
that heaven awaits them (1 John 5:11).

The freedom we experience in this type of new normal should
not be used as a license to feed harmful physical desires, however.
Instead, we are to put our freedom to good use by humbly serving
others (Galatians 5:13). Let the difficulties of your past become your
testimony. And be prepared to tell others when they ask about the
hope you carry with you (1 Peter 3:15).

Jesus replied, "Very truly I tell you, no one can see the kingdom of
God unless they are born again." "How can someone be born when
they are old?" Nicodemus asked. "Surely they cannot enter a second
time into their mother's womb to be born!" Jesus answered, . . .
"Flesh gives birth to flesh, but the Spirit gives birth to spirit." (John
3:3–6)

"To those who believed in his name, he gave the right to become children of God—children born not of natural descent, nor of human decision or a husband's will, but born of God." (John 1:12–13)

Therefore, if anyone is in Christ, the new creation has come: The old has gone, the new is here! (2 Corinthians 5:17)

SIXTEEN

Discovering Your Purpose

FOR THE LAST twenty years or so, I'd ordered my life in such a way as to maximize my success and happiness. You can understand then why I became distressed when I began to watch it unravel. For ten of those years, I managed the highly successful assembly division of our company. I enjoyed going to work every day and completing a series of tasks necessary to keep my department running smoothly. It brought me tremendous satisfaction to oversee a half dozen supervisors as they labored to meet our daily shipment schedule. The previous year, we'd processed more than twenty-five million camera chassis. I was extremely proud of everything we accomplished.

The job I loved, one I naively imagined I'd be doing for decades, now belonged to someone else. My transfer out of the assembly division had nothing to do with job performance. In fact, just the opposite was true.

Our customers found themselves in a price war with their competition and were forced to slash prices of their one-time-use cameras to maintain market share. As their supplier, we were expected to pass significant cost savings on to them every year. We received only about twenty-five cents for our part of the process for a camera selling for about ten dollars. My boss characterized our cost reduction efforts as "trying to squeeze blood from a stone." Our company sales dwindled rapidly when our customer decided to move their camera business to other countries where labor was cheaper.

To make up for our company's lost sales, we moved to an e-commerce business model. Website design, and online inventory management and reporting were going to be the salvation of our company. Since I had great success managing the assembly depart-ment and had recently obtained a master's degree, I was "promoted" to a sales support role called a Solutions Architect. I can remember thinking to myself, *Someone must have stayed up all night coming up with that job title.*

I knew nothing about web development and faced a steep learning curve. Our sales force was already at work promoting our new business model and communicated to our customers there was no limit to what we could do for them. It became my responsibility to make sure these promises were implemented. While it was exciting to be a pioneer in a new field, I found the work highly stressful.

Patty's job also changed. She transitioned from midnights to working day hours. Her new hours added tasks to my morning routine. It became my responsibility to get the boys on the school bus the days she was working.

Patty and I were also splitting time trying to teach our sons how to drive a car. Though it was a big help signing them up for driver education classes at school, this was one more event on our already busy calendar. When they finally got their licenses, we had to endure a learning curve that included what the boys called "mistakes." I called them accidents.

One event I had no answer for was the day my father learned he had prostate cancer. The news hit me especially hard because he and I had recently worked through some relationship issues. I felt closer to him now than ever before, and I feared what cancer might do to him.

My routine with Lucky brought me a measure of sanity as life continued to drag me down an unpredictable path. I could count on him lingering at the table with drool dripping from his mouth while he waited for the little bit of milk I left behind in my cereal bowl. After breakfast, he kept pace with me while I scurried around the house making sure the boys were up and ready in time for the school bus. He sounded the alarm when the yellow box on wheels stopped at the end of our driveway. Before I left for work, Lucky was the last one I said good-bye to as I put him in his pen. He never lost that fearful look in his eyes when I closed him in.

In the afternoon, when the boys got home from school, one of them would let Lucky out of his pen. They were usually too busy with homework or talking with their friends on the phone to pay much attention to him. Lucky bided his time, resting on the ottoman and looking out the living room window. He was waiting for one thing—my Chevy Blazer to appear in the driveway.

When the garage door opener roared to life, Lucky sprang from the ottoman and waited for me by the kitchen door with his tail wagging. He allowed Patty and me to embrace before begging for my attention. I rewarded his vigilance by offering him a hug. Flush with enthusiasm, he tailgated me from the coat closet to the bedroom where he waited for me to change clothes.

Lucky's anticipation grew as I changed into the real version of me outfitted in jeans and a T-shirt. He waited impatiently, shifting his weight back and forth on his front paws, reseating himself every few seconds. His tail thumped on the floor when I reached in a drawer and pulled out a pair of white cotton socks. He totally lost it when he saw me put on my sneakers.

Lucky barked and ran laps between his leash, which was draped over the railing by the front door, and my bedroom. He communicated with his body the words he desperately wanted to say. It was impossible to ignore his message.

My sidekick and I usually had enough time for a walk around the block while Patty put the finishing touches on supper. I welcomed the fresh air in my lungs, while Lucky chased the scents of untold creatures with his nose. He didn't pull me down the road like he once did, even though his enthusiasm remained unchanged. In the evening

Patty and I retired to the living room where we watched television or worked on one of our many hobbies.

My latest hobby, genealogy, had been the healing balm that enabled me to engage in a better relationship with my father. As a child I aspired to be like him. Mom once told me that when I was born, he was so excited because he'd always wanted a son. I'm certain it pained him to watch me grow distant as the years passed by. Personal success clouded my eyes and caused me to question the relevance of his ways. My journey back in time with Dad led to some amazing historical discoveries. At the same time, it restored my adoration for him.

I'd been doing some soul searching for the past year or so. My past successes felt more like hollow victories when I considered the uncertainties swirling around me. In my prayers I asked God to show me what had gone wrong. The more I leaned on my faith, the more my perspective changed. I saw God's hand at work virtually everywhere I looked. I came to the realization I hadn't achieved success entirely on my own. Acknowledging God's involvement in my life brought me an epiphany. If God was actively involved in orchestrating my past success, then I could count on him to direct my future.

As the events of my life played themselves out day after day, I no longer felt like I was striving in vain. God's plan for my life was unfolding though I did not know where it would ultimately lead. Somewhere along the way Lucky became the companion I had hoped for. With the rest of my family involved with their commitments, Lucky kept me grounded. Because of that I looked for ways to reward him.

Lucky enjoyed peanut butter as much as I did. Whenever I made a peanut butter and jelly sandwich, I saved some of the crust for him. If I emptied a plastic peanut butter jar, I handed it to Lucky. He treasured every bit of peanut butter that remained in the container and was determined to lick it spotless. Giving the jar to Lucky, however, got *me* in trouble.

"Bill!" Patty hollered.

"Yes?"

"Can you come here for a minute?"

"What's up?" I said, joining her in the living room.

"Why do you keep giving Lucky empty peanut butter jars?"

"Because he loves them."

Judging from Patty's expression, it wasn't the answer she was looking for.

"Is there a problem?"

"See for yourself," Patty responded, gesturing to the pool of vomit in the center of the room. "He is swallowing pieces of the plastic, and that can't be good for him."

"I'll clean it up. Where is he, by the way?"

"He's hiding behind the end table."

There were more chewed pieces of jar scattered around Lucky where he lay. He was still working hard at getting every little bit out of the bottom of the jar.

"Give it to me, Lucky."

Sheepishly, he complied and followed me into the kitchen. I was as determined to give him an opportunity to finish the job, so I sawed the jar in half using a serrated kitchen knife. Now he could reach the bottom of the container with ease. I managed a smile watching Lucky stretch out by the back door gleefully licking the peanut butter off the bottom of the jar. He never chewed another jar after that.

Late in July we spent the afternoon and evening hours in the hospital waiting to hear the outcome of Dad's cancer surgery. The surgeon looked exhausted after the surgery and offered little in the way of hope. Apparently, he'd encountered more cancer than he expected. Dad spent a week in the hospital recovering from his surgery. It was hard to think about anything else during that time. The only thing I could do was pray for his recovery.

While Dad was sidelined, I got involved in some of the projects around his house. This meant spending less time with Lucky. Because of that I relished every opportunity I had to play with him. He coveted the Frisbee, while I coveted the fresh air. I trusted him to stay beside me as we walked around the yard. If I had the flying disc in my hand, I believed he would follow me anywhere.

Patty thought I was crazy for not putting him on a leash. She didn't think it was a good idea to give him that much freedom. She'd witnessed what Lucky had done with his freedom. I gave her credit for being right about a lot of things, but I was Lucky's owner. Besides, Miss D's Great Danes were no longer something we had to contend with, which added to my confidence level. One of her dogs had died, and she kept the other one inside most of the time because it had hip issues.

Our playtime in the backyard that day began like any other time we played with the Frisbee. An errant throw landed the Frisbee in one of Miss D's evergreens, but I was certain Lucky would dislodge it and play would resume. He had always done so in the past. I was caught completely off guard, however, when Lucky ignored it and bolted into her backyard. He never stopped running and disappeared around the corner of Miss D's house before I could react. From the speed he was traveling, he could be anywhere in the neighborhood by the time I made it to Miss D's front yard. Disappointed, I kicked the sod. It was almost time for supper, and the last thing I felt like doing was chasing Lucky around the neighborhood.

I felt a sense of relief when he suddenly reappeared on the opposite side of Miss D's house and was headed back in my direction. I was mystified as to why he was acting the way he was.

"Lucky, come here! Now!" I shouted, trying to get him to obey.

He never looked up; he just kept on running with his nose to the ground. Lucky had completely circled Miss D's house and was about to start another lap. What on earth was he doing? And why wasn't he listening to me? It was the thought of one of my neighbors saying "Look at that fool chasing his dog" that kept me from immediately going after him.

Lucky had already completed a second lap while I was pondering what to do. I fought my way through the densely packed row of trees separating our backyards, thinking I would be close enough to grab him when he passed by. It was then that I spotted a freshly dug hole in front of Miss D's deck skirting. I attributed the burrow to a rabbit because I had seen one in our front yard recently.

"Lucky, come here!" I yelled.

No response. He whizzed by me again before I could grab him. Desperate to put an end to this nonsense, I decided to put myself directly in his path the next time he came around. Surely that would get his attention. Like clockwork, Lucky reappeared again. Contrary to what he believed, there was no rabbit running around Miss D's house out in front of him. Nothing I said or did was going to convince him otherwise, so I picked a spot to stand and squatted down to his eye level. It crossed my mind that it might not be a good idea to be standing in his path. I was about to play chicken with a sprinting seventy-pound dog.

"Lucky!"

A moment before the impact, I caught a rare glimpse into the all-consuming nature of desire. He was caught in its grip and oblivious to me as I begged him to stop before someone got hurt. The resulting collision was painful. His bony head hit me squarely on the jaw and laid me out flat on my back. I grabbed his collar as he attempted to run over me.

I slowly picked myself up off the ground, shaking my head in disbelief.

"What is wrong with you?" I said.

He appeared unfazed by the collision. Thankfully, I accomplished my objective of corralling him. I quicky escorted him into the house.

At the dinner table that evening Patty caught me rubbing my chin.

"What's wrong?" she asked.

"I bumped into Lucky," I replied, leaving out the part about Lucky taking off on me.

Being able to get away on weekends also played a big part in helping me deal with the stress I was under. One of our favorite jaunts was staying at a Christian campground located on the shores of Lake Ontario. The more we visited the campground, the more we fell in love with the place.

We ended up leasing an RV site about a dozen lots down from my parents' cottage. Carlin and Sandy's graciously parked their truck camper on our site. Patty and I drank in the peaceful and relaxing atmosphere. Being away from all the distractions at home meant we could spend time together as a family.

Patty's father donated his old boat to me, which added to our fun. It was the very same boat I kidded him about being seaworthy years earlier. I worried that the craft might not be reliable enough on a lake as large as Ontario, so I spent a considerable amount of time refurbishing the engine. Before long, I was proudly cruising back and forth on the lake in front of the campground. We brought Lucky along whenever we went for the ride. He rode with his tongue flopping in the breeze, gulping in the fresh air. Occasionally, he'd drape his front paws over the side of the boat to get a better view. Our vessel enabled us to go sightseeing, waterskiing, or tubing whenever the mood hit us.

One afternoon in late August the humidity was so high my clothes were sticking to me. The temperature had eclipsed ninety degrees. We didn't have air conditioning in the camper and the shade was doing nothing to keep us cool. But what we did have was the lake, and the water was as calm as I'd ever seen it. I rounded up Dan and Mike while Patty packed the cooler. We planned to eat supper out on the water.

I hurriedly launched the boat and we all piled in. Moments later we were gliding over the surface of the water heading east as fast as the engine would take us. We took in the sights along the shoreline, which included a water level view of the thirty-mile-point lighthouse. Eventually we reversed course and headed back toward the campground. The clouds popped with color as the sun inched closer to the horizon. The only breeze available to us was the one the boat created as it skimmed over the water's surface.

Our mini adventure was so inspiring that it caused me to act spontaneously, something I never did, let alone in a boat on a big lake. While no one was watching, I killed the engine. It immediately got deathly quiet as the boat glided to a stop. A look of concern grew on Patty's face.

"Bill, is everything all right?" Patty asked, knowing the boat was almost as old as she was.

"I thought it might be a good time to take a swim."

"Here? Now?"

"Why not?"

Dan and Mike looked at me like I'd lost my mind when I jumped overboard wearing my swim trunks and ski vest. We were about seventy-five yards from shore, and the water was so calm I never bothered to put down an anchor. I figured we could swim to shore if the boat failed to start. Patty gave me a wide smile and shook her head.

"Why not?" Patty said and lowered herself gently over the side. "Hey, the water is pretty warm."

Dan and Mike were not about to be outdone and joined us with cannonball splashes. Together we drank in the sunset while we bobbed on the water. In that moment I was reminded of my purpose in life: to be a good husband and father to my family. That moment, nothing else seemed important.

Lucky paced nervously back and forth in the abandoned vessel. What troubled him was something that concerns all of us from time to time—he felt left out.

"Come on, Lucky," I said.

It took some convincing, but eventually he entered the water with a splash. He bobbed on the surface for a moment, and then in duck like fashion he paddled over to me. The incident earned him a new nickname, Lucky Ducky.

We continued visiting our campsite late into October. The mature maple and beech trees were radiant with color. Late corn and wheat in the farmers' fields surrounding the campground were in the process of being harvested. It was a magnificent time to be alive. Most of the cottages were vacant this time of year, so I was able to let Lucky roam free on occasion when I took a walk.

Lucky ran back and forth out ahead of me on the private gravel roadways. He chased the scents of squirrels and rabbits to his heart's content. When Patty and I walked along the lakeshore, Lucky ran ahead of us, stopping to sniff around the large piles of loose stones that make up the shoreline. I stopped occasionally to skip a flat stone on the waves. Lucky sometimes plunged into the water after it but exited quickly when the stone disappeared beneath the surface of the waves.

When Christmas morning arrived, I knew it held special significance because I didn't know how many more Dad would have with us. Patty and I opened our presents at home with the boys that morning before piling into the Blazer and heading to my parents' house for brunch.

In our haste to leave, we neglected to pen up Lucky. During the fifteen-minute ride, we argued over whose fault it was. When the point was made that Lucky was my dog, I deemed no further discussion was necessary. We shifted our focus to having a wonderful time eating with my parents and opening presents. I completely forgot about Lucky.

When we returned home, I opened the kitchen door and Lucky was not there to greet us. He was trapped upstairs behind the hallway door and in full panic mode, barking and clawing as if his life depended on it. My mind flashed back to the note we received years ago from his previous owners. A sick feeling grew in my stomach as I sprinted up the stairs.

I opened the door and Lucky shot past me like he'd just been released from prison. Pieces of weatherstripping lay on the floor in front of me. It seemed clear my fear was justified. I recently invested a lot of time and money finishing off the upstairs of our Cape Cod. I was proud of my achievement, having added two new bedrooms and a bathroom for the boys. I didn't have to look very far to see more damage. The words Patty uttered back when Lucky came to stay with us proved to be prophetic: "He will destroy this house if we don't pen him up."

The brand-new carpet I paid to have installed was shredded in one corner. Lucky had added to the damage by pulling off sections of door casing and making deep gouges in the drywall adjacent to the door. Thankfully, the door itself remained intact.

I descended the stairs full of disappointment. I didn't bother to say anything to Lucky when I let him outside into the kennel. I could argue all day whose fault it was, but what purpose would that serve? The damage was done. When I compared my loss to what my father must be going through, mine seemed trivial. I could fix the damage upstairs, but I didn't know if the doctors could fix my dad.

~

Discovering Your Purpose

After Dad was diagnosed with cancer, I spent as much time with him that my schedule would allow. He loved it when I took time to brief him on the most recent family history finds. Perhaps he took comfort in knowing that our ancestors were remembered as godly men and women. They would not be forgotten, and neither would he. Lucky accompanied me on a few visits to see Dad. He turned out to be a decent therapy dog. I'd forgotten how much my father loved dogs.

I journaled my remaining time with Dad. My thoughts were captured in the book *Junior's Hope: A Memoir of a Father's Son*. My father succumbed to his cancer and joined Jesus in heaven. Deep down inside I knew God had called me to my father's side for a special purpose (Jeremiah 15:11). I watched that purpose gradually be revealed as time passed. Perhaps I was the answer to Dad's prayer for help (Hebrews 6:10). As I journeyed through those turbulent years, I learned a thing or two about divine providence.

For me providence took on a special meaning: "to provide evidence." My experience taught me that providence wasn't solely about enduring Dad's illness, job stress, or any of the other hardships I faced. During those times, I trained my spiritual eyes to watch for evidence of God's hand at work (John 14:11). When I saw the evidence, it served to steel my faith. A measure of peace followed when I realized God was going to be at work in my future endeavors as well.

I was fortunate to have Lucky with me in the months that followed Dad's passing. There were times when I found myself alone and anxiety made its bid to overwhelm me. Lucky, faults and all, was there with me—the orphaned creature who had become my friend.

God in His ultimate wisdom and perfect timing placed this creature in my path well before I needed him. I learned God can, and will, use less than perfect people, objects, and circumstances to guide me to Himself. God wanted me to involve Him in times of suffering as well as those moments when happiness abounds.

Who but God could take a waterlogged puppy, abandoned shortly after its birth, and keep him alive long enough to be rescued? Who but God could create the necessary circumstances for his rescuer to place that puppy for adoption? Who but God could prepare me ahead of time to receive an imperfect companion plagued by destructive behavior? Lucky was created for a purpose—to be my friend. Lucky's life mattered to God.

I catch myself wondering why God chose to use a dog to help me as I journeyed. Maybe it's because dogs have the capability to love completely someone other than themselves. Life is a joy to a dog and worth living no matter what happens along the way. They understand what it means to be a companion and are willing to make the necessary sacrifices.

God used my love for dogs to demonstrate how much He loves me. The traits that make a dog special are the same traits that make me special to God. My relationship with Him will flourish if I trust Him completely. It was for this purpose I was created. My life matters to God.

Then Job replied to the LORD: "I know that you can do all things; no purpose of yours can be thwarted. You asked, 'Who is this who obscures my plans without knowledge?' Surely I spoke of things I did not understand, things too wonderful to know. You said, 'Listen

now, and I will speak; I will question you, and you will answer me.'
My ears had heard of you but now my eyes have seen you." (Job
42:1–5)

Many are the plans in a person's heart, but it is the LORD's purpose
that prevails. (Proverbs 19:21)

What, then, shall we say in response to these things? If God is for us,
who can be against us? (Romans 8:31)

SEVENTEEN

Good and Faithful Servant

MY THIRTY-TWO-YEAR CAREER at the plastics factory that began when I was sixteen came to an end when I found work as a custodial supervisor at my church. It was a huge relief to be rid of the job stress I'd carried on my shoulders. It was a pleasure to do physical work with my hands again. I rediscovered the joy of making a lasting difference in the lives of those working under me. The handful of workers I supervised were taught more than just cleaning methods. They learned they were serving God when they cleaned. I fell in love with the work I was doing.

I felt like a different person after my father died. Imagine my surprise when I discovered I was the patriarch of my father's lineage. I didn't know what I was supposed to do with that piece of information, and I hoped none of my family members came to me for advice.

My appreciation for my loved ones grew exponentially. I quit suppressing the tender feelings I had for others. Hugs became voguish, and my eyes welled with tears when I saw compassionate acts being portrayed on the silver screen. Dan and Mike, though they were now college students living on campus, could not escape my declarations of love. Because I called on God as I grieved, He faithfully met my need. I found a measure of peace that was hard to put into words (Romans 15:13).

Patty and I offered to host my extended family for Thanksgiving dinner. It was a pleasure to invite them into our home. Patty agreed to host provided I carved the turkey, something my father had always done in the past. Family members brought dishes to share and offered to lend a hand cleaning up afterwards. I looked forward to having a grand time.

Lucky, however, almost wrecked the event. He sat by the table and drooled profusely as the food was being passed. His slobber accumulated in small pools on the floor and ended up on people's clothes when he rubbed up against them seeking attention. It was embarrassing.

When Patty gave me that determined look on her face, I knew she wanted me to do something. I tried to solve the problem by putting Lucky out in the garage. But he didn't want to be excluded from the party. He clawed so intensely at the door frame that he ruined the magnetic seal on the weatherstripping. I tried to ignore him. He resorted to barking nonstop when I didn't let him back in.

Patty nudged me under the table with her foot. My frustration with Lucky grew while Patty maintained the pleasant smile of a hostess. I decided to take a chance on shutting Lucky in Patty's van. Scenes from the movie *Turner and Hooch* flashed through my mind as I closed him in. In the movie, Hooch, a dog, shredded the upholstery in Turner's car while he was locked inside. I told myself, *That was just a movie.*

I reseated myself at the table believing I had found the solution. Just as I was about to take a bite of my rapidly cooling dinner, Lucky started barking again. When his barking reached a fever pitch, I caught Patty's attention and mouthed the words, "I don't know what else to do." She mouthed back, "Figure it out."

I considered locking him outside in the kennel, but it was a cold day, and I didn't want to burden my neighbors with his barking on Thanksgiving. Lucky finally got what he wanted when I put him on a leash and fastened it to the doorknob in the kitchen. There he could watch us eat and drool all he wanted while I ate a cold turkey dinner.

After Thanksgiving, we had a stretch of Indian summer which inspired Patty and me to work out in the garage. She pawed through the storage bin looking for items we no longer used, fueled by the notion that we could start thinning out our belongings now that the boys were gone.

"Bill, remember these," she said, holding a pair of rollerblades under my nose as I tried to drain the oil from the riding lawn mower.

"We didn't use them very much, did we? They'd make a good donation to the church's garage sale."

"You can donate yours. I have something planned for these."

"You're almost fifty. What are you going to do with them?"

"I thought it'd be fun to have Lucky pull me around the block."

"I don't think that's a good idea."

"Oh, don't be such a spoilsport."

Lucky had been keeping a close eye on Patty as she pawed through the sacred bin. He was hoping she might happen on a Frisbee. I warned her not to let him see one. Lucky barked and bounced up and down with excitement when I returned to the garage carrying his leash.

"Are you sure you want to do this?" I asked.

"I'll be fine."

Patty looked quite eye-catching donned in Rollerblades, white fitted jeans, and a sweatshirt. I talked her into wearing wrist guards and a bicycle helmet—"just in case." My roller derby queen wobbled down the driveway with Lucky leading the way. It didn't take long for her to find her stride. I reminded myself that our generation grew up on roller-skating socials. *She'll probably be okay.*

Lucky was unsure why Patty would ask him to pull on the leash after I spent years trying to get him to stop pulling. But with Patty's encouragement, he decided it was okay to let loose. Patty's occasional strides combined with Lucky pulling propelled the pair down the street. To my amazement, they safely negotiated the corner and disappeared out of sight.

I couldn't let go of the thought that something bad was about to happen. I toyed with the idea of getting on my bike in case Patty ran into difficulty. After all, Lucky was involved. I finally convinced myself I was acting too much like a nervous parent watching their child learn how to ride a bike. Patty was a grown woman, and her instincts were usually correct.

I added fresh oil to the lawn mower and fired it up. Mowing the lawn was a form of therapy for me. I often used the monotonous activity as a think tank. The only thoughts I could muster that day, however, involved Patty's safety.

It was too late in the year to mow, but I circled the house a couple of times to give the new oil time to work itself into the engine. I was headed into the backyard to stow the mower under the deck for the winter when Patty and Lucky came into view. I was amazed they made it all the way around. From the smile on her face, Patty appeared to be having a good time. She blew me a kiss, which I interpreted as "I told you I'd be okay." They didn't let up as they got near the driveway, so I figured they were going around a second time.

Out of the corner of my eye I saw something scamper across the street ahead of them. I wasn't the only one; Lucky saw it too. If there was one creature that excited him more than rabbits, it was squirrels. He barked himself silly when one of them invaded our yard.

What a fortunate turn of events this was for Lucky. He was outside and right where the action was. His eyes locked on the creature, completely disregarding the fact he was still pulling Patty.

The first thing they taught me when I first learned how to waterski was if you get in trouble, be sure to let go of the rope. I knew if I didn't let go, there was a good chance I'd get hurt.

"Let go of the leash!" I yelled.

Patty's mind was processing a different thought: *If I let go, Lucky will get away.*

She did an amazing job maintaining her balance following Lucky's jerk, which spun her ninety degrees. She even stayed on her feet when her Rollerblades dropped into the culvert. But skill and

poise could only take her so far. The instant the toe of her
Rollerblade touched the lawn, she looked like a cat falling out of the
tree with limbs sprawled out in every direction.

I jumped off the mower and rushed over to her, hoping I
wouldn't have to call the ambulance. Patty lay facedown and motionless in the lawn. After a moment of reflection, she rolled over and sat
up. She ripped off her wrist guards and helmet and cast them aside.

Once I knew she was okay, I couldn't keep myself from
laughing.

"I never saw that coming," she said, unbuckling her Rollerblades.
"I did."

Patty handed me the leash and rose to her feet. I heard her sigh
when she realized how badly her jeans were grass stained.

"What do you want me to do with your Rollerblades?" I asked.

"Whatever you want to," she replied as she walked back into the
house.

Lucky had treed the squirrel and wrapped his leash around the
base of the tree as he looked for it. It was one of the few times I can
remember Patty being wrong about Lucky, and I took great pleasure
in reminding her about it later.

Lucky and I continued to grow closer together despite his
sporadic moments of drama. My mind-set shifted from *Let's get this
walk over with* to *Where can Lucky and I walk today?* Our walks
grew longer and often stretched beyond the confines of our housing
development. Sometimes we walked on rural sideroads, and on other
occasions I drove to a park where we could explore nature trails
together. I knew he was prone to disappointing me, but that didn't
seem to bother me like it once did.

Early in December after playing Frisbee, I caught Lucky limping
around the house. In all the time I'd known him, I'd never seen him
limp. He was still lame the next day, so I surmised he'd tweaked a
muscle.

After two days he wasn't feeling any better. He whimpered when
he dragged himself to his feet and lacked his usual energy and determination.

"Are you okay, Lucky?"

A week later, his condition still hadn't improved, so I scheduled an appointment with the veterinarian. He'd lost his appetite, which caused his body to undergo a rapid change. His collar drooped from his neck like a necklace.

I lifted my dog of ten years onto the examining table. The vet recorded his weight as sixty-nine pounds, virtually the same weight as his last visit. Lucky remained calm and listless while the vet probed his sides.

"Lucky has a massive growth around his spleen," the vet said. "I suspect the spleen has ruptured and is allowing blood to seep out into his abdominal cavity."

"Is there anything that can be done for him?" I asked.

"Blood tests would confirm what I already know. He's anemic. Look at his gums."

The doctor rattled off some options that included ultrasound and surgery. He doubted they were realistic options, however, given the size of the mass. Even with surgery, the best-case scenario was about six months, and we'd have to restrict his activity. I knew that wasn't a realistic option because there was nothing about Lucky's life that fit the description of restricted.

I stood beside Lucky, feeling as helpless as the little boy holding his sick dog in the Norman Rockwell painting prominently displayed on the wall across from me. But *my* dog couldn't be fixed.

I brought Lucky home and wondered how much time he had left. I made up my mind Lucky and I would face his remaining days head-on. My father had shown me what courage looked like. I owed it to Lucky to be strong for him.

To my surprise, Lucky rallied over the next several days. His appetite and activity level approached normal. Not knowing what was going on inside his body, walks and playing catch with the Frisbee were not an option. Instead, I poured affection into him knowing he was on borrowed time. I gave him a Frisbee or tennis ball to keep him company while I was at work. He didn't disappoint me when I returned home each evening to find the objects permanently disabled.

Several days later, on a Friday morning, my heartache returned when I saw Lucky sprawled out on the living room floor. He didn't follow me around the house as I moved about during my morning routine. He just lay on the floor and listened. He managed to struggle to his feet when he heard me descend the basement stairs to my study, knowing I'd probably be there awhile. It dawned on me that Lucky was picking and choosing our last moments together.

With great difficulty he navigated the stairs and joined me, positioning himself on the cool basement floor where he could see me. I reached down and patted him on the head, my way of thanking him for making the effort to join me. When I looked into his eyes, his stare lacked the determination I was used to seeing. It seemed more to me one of longing, a desire for more time. I teared up when I wondered if he knew something was seriously wrong with him.

I felt a stirring desire to be closer to him, so I joined him on the cold cement floor and resumed my preparations for the class I was leading in church on Sunday morning.

His trek downstairs turned out to be a one-way trip. He lacked the strength to follow me upstairs when I left the room to refill my coffee mug. I spotted him lying at the bottom of the stairs when I came back to check on him. His head bobbed when he looked up, and he struggled to keep his eyes trained on me.

My heart was deeply burdened. I was quickly coming undone. If this was the end, the basement was not a suitable place for us to spend our remaining hours together. I struggled to pick him up, taking care not to hurt him. There was trust in his eyes when I cradled him like a lamb and climbed the stairs.

I couldn't remember if I had let him out that morning to go the bathroom, so I carried him out into the front yard. Lucky staggered around like he was heavily drugged. It took a considerable effort to work his way over to one of the shrubs. The very same shrubs he'd watered ten years earlier, the day I brought him home.

My mind raced, nostalgic thoughts mixed with tears. My once

chiseled and athletic companion now struggled to stand. I carried Lucky back inside and laid him gently on a blanket. Not knowing what else to do, I called Patty and told her what was happening. She understood his time had come.

Lucky faced me while I talked to Patty. I didn't see a bit of fear in his eyes. It was more like disappointment, or maybe regret. It was as if he was wrestling with the thought that he'd have to leave me. I hoped I had given him everything an adopted dog could ask for—a new home, a new life, and lots of love. Somehow I think he knew and appreciated that.

When the vet receptionist learned the reason for my call, her sympathy was palpable. Her compassion sent me to the edge of hysteria. It was like she reached into the depths of my soul and guided out my grief. I was crying so hard I could barely communicate with her. Part of me wished she would curtly tell me to "get a hold of yourself!" Maybe then I could have stopped crying.

Seeing Lucky stretched out on the blanket, resting his head between his paws, broke my heart. Strength was rapidly leaving his body, yet he refused to close his eyes and rest. Instead, he kept his eyes fixed on me as if vowing to do so.

There was nothing more exciting to Lucky than having his leash brought to him. In the past, his reaction was the equivalent of turning over the engine of a high-performance car. Without thinking, Lucky leaped to his feet, an adrenaline-induced act. He staggered, then hesitated, unsure if he'd be able to walk. He once again welcomed my gesture to carry him. Going for a car ride was also near the top of the list of his favorite things, but he couldn't even bring himself to wag his tail when I placed him on the backseat.

I carried him inside the vet's office for the second time in two weeks and stood at the front desk signing his life over to be euthanized. Tears stained the paper I was trying to write on. I didn't want the responsibility to take his life from him.

The ten-minute wait seemed like an hour. I watched in agony as Lucky struggled to bear his weight on his front legs while he sat. His legs kept sliding out from underneath him on the tiled floor. When I couldn't bear to watch him struggle any longer, I picked him up and gathered him into my lap. I couldn't stop my mind from reminiscing.

I pictured Lucky waiting for me to come home, greeting me like the hero who refused to abandon him. I held him closer to let him know I was with him now. Even though playtime was often on his terms, I couldn't thank him enough for helping me relive the glory days I once had with Sheba. Watching him catch the Frisbee was a thing of beauty. His antics brought me laughter: running into me when I tried to stop him from chasing a rabbit, boat rides, watching him pull Patty down the street on her Rollerblades. I loved seeing people react to Lucky sitting in the driver's seat and looking out over the steering wheel. "That's my dog," I told them. I loved watching him run free on the campground, which now seemed like an image one would find in heaven.

When the vet came for him, I lacked the courage to go with him into the examining room. Instead, I set Lucky gently on the tile floor and knelt face-to-face with him. I stroked his ears and looked into his eyes one last time before I said good-bye. I hoped he would under-stand why I couldn't go in and watch him die. With all the strength he could muster, he rose to his feet and tested each step before taking another one. Moments later he was gone.

In the days that passed, our house was quieter than I could ever remember it being. I missed the uniqueness Lucky brought to our home. Everywhere I looked, I was reminded of him: the kennel, the bin of sporting goods, coverless tennis balls, unusable Frisbees, and the ottoman where I rested my feet every day. It didn't feel right having the entire ottoman to myself. I knew in my heart there would never be another dog like him.

I went to church on Sunday dreading the fact that I would be in front of a group of people to present a lesson on the book of Ephesians. My mind wanted desperately to be somewhere else. I decided I'd better let them know what was going on. I hoped they would understand the struggle I was having. At the suggestion of someone in the class, we stopped and prayed for the heaviness resting on my heart. With God's help I was able to make it through the lesson.

Jim, a man I had known for a couple of years, approached me after class and told me with all sincerity he believed God was going to turn my grief into a special blessing. I appreciated his kind words. When I got home, I tried to figure out what he meant by "a special blessing." Unfortunately, nothing came to mind.

~

Good and Faithful Servant

When I think of a good and faithful servant, I imagine someone committed to performing acts of kindness for someone else regardless of the character of the recipient. *Servant* is one of the most prolific words in Scripture. It appears more than 450 times in the *New International Version* of the Bible. A good portion of those references had to do with the culture of that day, one that practiced slavery.

Jesus took the graphic imagery of a slave and gave it a new meaning: a man or woman who professed to have a relationship with Him. Someone freed from the bondage of sin who willingly engaged in a lifestyle of servitude toward others (Matthew 20:26–28). Those who called themselves servants of God were acting as ambassadors for his Son, Jesus (2 Corinthians 5:20). Followers of Jesus can love others because God first loved them (1 John 4:19). When they perform good deeds, they are casting a bright light to shine in a dark world (Matthew 5:16).

I struggled with titling this chapter "Good and Faithful Servant." At first glance, comparing Lucky to a good and faithful servant seemed like comparing the behavior of an arrogant cat to that of a devoted dog. Lucky fell somewhere in the middle. It was when I compared Lucky's struggles with servanthood to mine that I found common ground. Lucky taught me that servanthood doesn't have to be complicated. It can be as simple as being there for someone when they need you.

I am a broken person living in a broken world. Selfish behavior was a protection mechanism Lucky and I used to shield us from our fears. If we became a servant in a broken world, that would leave us exposed and vulnerable. That's where love comes in. Perfect love in the hearts of a good and faithful servant enables them to cast fear aside (1 John 4:18).

The memory of Lucky reminds me I must not let mistakes or failures disqualify me from what God has called me to do. Love is a fragrant balm that treats brokenness, and confession is the means to remove guilty stains. Those who commit themselves to God will one day hear the words, "Well done, good and faithful servant."

Above all, love each other deeply, because love covers over a multitude of sins. Offer hospitality to one another without grumbling. Each of you should use whatever gift you have received to serve others, as faithful stewards of God's grace in its various forms. (1 Peter 4:8–10)

"For even the Son of Man did not come to be served, but to serve, and to give his life as a ransom for many." (Mark 10:45)

"His master replied, 'Well done, good and faithful servant! You have been faithful with a few things; I will put you in charge of many things. Come and share your master's happiness!'" (Matthew 25:21)

EIGHTEEN

Devotion
_____

I DROVE past a towering oak tree on my commute to work. The late afternoon sun brushed an otherwise drab trunk with streaks of gold. Heavy limbs branched out from its mammoth trunk and stretched upward, scraping the turquoise sky. I missed the tangerine leaves that had simmered in the autumn breezes just a few short weeks ago. They fell and were scattered far from their home. Like the mighty oak, I was preparing myself for the ravages of winter with nothing but bare branches.

Our house was ghostly quiet. The laughter and drama that once flickered and danced like the flame of a candle was snuffed out under the weight of Lucky's passing. Dan's and Mike's rooms lay dormant. Now graduates, they moved out to meet life on their own terms. Patty and I were saddened by their departure, but we thanked God they felt confident enough to stand on their own.

As I looked at my life, I realized I had traveled in a big circle. In many respects I was back where I'd started twenty-six years ago. Back then, Patty and I lived in a house with no children under our roof. Similarly, our work schedules barely overlapped, forcing us to spend most of the day apart. I noted that God provided us with Sheba to fill that void once upon a time.

From my vantage point, life felt like a do-over. I was a pilgrim walking down a familiar road, carrying past life experiences with me. I called on God to point out anything I might have missed out on the first time around, and I prayed He would keep me pointed in the right direction.

Experience nudged me into considering another dog, a companion to keep me company while Patty was working. The plan worked once; why not try it again? I didn't want just any dog this time around, however. I wanted one that was affectionate and train-able like Lady, a devoted protector like Sheba, with a touch of Lucky's zest for life thrown in. I guess you could say I missed all my dogs.

Patty didn't need much convincing. She understood how much I loved dogs and offered her opinion on the matter. "Could we get a smaller one this time?" From her perspective, a smaller dog would be easier to handle and clean up after. Personally, I wanted to stay away from an older one because I didn't want to mourn another loss anytime soon.

Armed with these thoughts, I contacted a couple animal shelters in our area. We'd had reasonable success adopting Lucky, so it seemed like a logical place to start. The first two shelters I contacted only had large animals, so I kept looking.

I finally found a shelter that had a dog we might be interested in. His name was Maximus. *What a catchy name,* I thought. I was willing to bet his previous owner was a fan of the movie *Gladiator* and named him after its main character.

The woman on the phone described Maximus as a medium-size dog, and although she didn't know his exact age, she believed he was a younger animal. I relayed the news to Patty, and we agreed to consider him for adoption. Their policy stated that if for any reason the dog wasn't a good fit, we could return him to the shelter.

I took Friday off work so Patty and I could introduce ourselves to Maximus. From the looks of him, he was a downsized version of a Husky. He had a beautiful coat, a mixture of white, grey, and sandy-brown hues. He seemed friendly enough when we interacted with him, so we agreed to take him home with us on a trial basis.

It was as if someone had fired a starter's pistol when I unclipped his leash in the living room. Maximus sprinted in and out of every room of the house, expending the most energy in the living room. While there, he bounded from one piece of furniture to another. Since our "wild thing" didn't know the house rules, Patty and I extended him some grace. There was really nothing else we could do until he learned the "get down" command.

His crazy pace eventually slowed enough for me to lead him to his food and water bowls in the kitchen. He ate and drank ravenously. I used the opportunity to clip his leash back on. After all that water, it seemed like the perfect time to introduce him to our yard. Better yet, a walk around the block might reduce his energy to a more manageable level.

Lucky set the bar so low when it came to learning how to walk on a leash that anything Maximus did was bound to be an improvement. As it turned out, Maximus was a better walker in all but one respect. His pace was so brisk that I had to walk at a faster pace than I was comfortable with. I worried that if I broke into a jog, Maximus would be inclined to pick up the pace even further.

While we were out walking, Kit came across Maximus's scent as he wandered through the house. He was intrigued. *Who was this foreigner?* Our feline delicately sniffed the floor, probing it an inch at a time with his nose. Kit tracked the scent up onto the sofa. *I thought dogs weren't allowed on the sofa.* He purred to himself, as if processing the thought.

I burst in the front door with Maximus and caught Kit completely by surprise. Had I known he was in the living room, I would have done a better job of trying to hold on to the leash. Maximus went berserk when he spotted the cat. He lunged forward, yanking the leash out of my hand. Only God knows what he was thinking. Did he want a friendly sniff or an early dinner? Either way, Kit was on his own. Without the leash, I could do nothing to halt the dog's charge.

Maximus reached the couch in a matter of seconds. But Kit had already abandoned the sofa by the time he got there. I rarely rooted for cats, but I feared for Kit's life. Our feline sprinted for the cellar door as if his life depended on it. An equally fast and determined Maximus gave chase. Had it not been for the flap I'd installed on the cellar door years earlier, Kit would have been cornered. Patty dashed out of our bedroom when she heard the commotion. Neither of us were laughing as we stared at each other.

I knew this was a serious matter, but I also didn't want to overreact. Maximus had only been with us for a little over an hour. It seemed like chaos had reigned the entire time. I was thankful Kit was safe for the time being. Feeling exhausted, I led Maximus to the kitchen where his new accommodations awaited him. He walked straight into the pen like it was the most natural thing in the world. I marveled at the sight. Lucky never willingly entered his pen.

"Good boy, Maximus," I said.

I collapsed in my favorite chair in the living room and drank in the quietness surrounding me. It wasn't long before I heard Patty climbing the basement stairs. She peeked around the corner to see what I was up to. When I saw the stack of clean clothes from the laundry room in her arms, I realized the bundle she carried was used as a pretense to go check on Kit.

I gazed out the window watching the afternoon shadows lengthen and second-guessing myself. *Was it too soon to be thinking about getting another dog?* More thoughts followed. I willed myself to push the negative thoughts out of my mind. *It's too soon to judge Maximus. We're just getting to know him.*

I heard Patty moving pans around in the kitchen and decided to join her.

"Do I dare ask what you think of him so far?" I asked.

"To be honest, I really don't know," Patty replied.

"That thing with the cat was scary."

"You don't think he would have hurt Kit, do you?"

"I have no idea. I was just as worried as you were," I confessed. "Why don't I take Maximus for another walk before it gets too dark."

"Please do! Dinner should be ready by the time you get back."

"Just remember, if we're not in agreement, then we won't keep him."

I gave Patty a hug because it looked like she desperately needed one.

Maximus sat quietly on the tile floor while Patty and I ate dinner. He didn't whine or drool, which impressed me a lot. After we finished eating, I led Maximus to his pen. I just couldn't get over how easy it was to coax him inside. It must be an animal shelter thing.

I bid him good night and turned out the kitchen lights, letting him know it was time for bed. Once in the living room, I turned on the television, thinking a little background noise would make him feel more at home. It wouldn't be quiet in an animal shelter.

A short time later Patty entered the darkened kitchen. Light leaked in from the living room, giving her silhouette definition. Maximus, seeing a figure approach, began to growl. Patty figured she must have startled him, so she turned on the light over the stove before approaching him. She offered an open palm for him to sniff. It was a gesture intending to reassure him he had nothing to worry about. Maximus rose to his feet and bared his teeth at Patty as she drew near. His growl intensified as she stood beside the pen, letting her know, "That's close enough."

Patty was one of the kindest people I knew. She'd go out of her way to make an earthworm feel welcome. Well, on second thought, maybe not an earthworm. She plopped down on the ottoman and stared directly into my face. I knew it was not a romantic gesture because of the fiery, determined look in her eyes.

"Bill, he can't stay here."

"What's wrong?"

"Didn't you hear him growling? He bared his teeth at me when I tried to be friendly."

"Are you serious?"

"I think he would have bitten me if I stuck my hand in the pen."

"Wow. He seemed okay a few minutes ago."

I knew Patty. It wasn't in her nature to deliberately try to sabotage my attempt to adopt a dog. But there was no point of keeping him if Patty didn't feel safe around him. We already knew he was going to be a handful. I conceded Maximus wasn't going to be a good fit for us. Our attempt wasn't completely wasted, however. I realized I wasn't ready for another long-term project like Lucky.

The next morning, I took Maximus out for one more walk before loading him in the car and returning him to the animal shelter. I apologized to him the entire drive, knowing full well everyone has baggage they carry around with them. Maximus was no different. Patty and I just weren't up for the challenge.

The lady behind the counter announced Maximus's return to her coworkers, who were somewhere in the back. She reminded me of a waitress shouting to a short-order cook when she yelled, "Maximus is back!"

I explained to her what happened, but she didn't seem surprised by it. Apparently, the woman who attempted to adopt Maximus before we did had a similar experience. I left the shelter feeling sad for Maximus, but I knew we made the right decision.

I thought about my experience with Maximus for several days. It took that long just to shake off my cold feet. It finally dawned on me that we should be looking for a puppy. It would require the same amount of effort for Patty and me to get used to a puppy. Yes, housebreaking was another story, but we'd been through that experience before. I sprang the idea on Patty. The thought of a fresh new start appealed to her.

I wasn't going to find a puppy at an animal shelter, however. I'd been checking their inventory of dogs regularly. I began sharing information with Patty daily that I pulled off the internet. On one of those days, I rattled off the ten most popular dog breeds, thinking maybe we should consider one of them. Patty grew up with beagles. My family had dachshunds. Both breeds made the top ten list: beagles fifth and dachshunds seventh. I jokingly told her this was the type of information that reinforced the idea that I married above my station. She playfully poked a finger in my chest and said, "You did, didn't you?"

I had to say I was surprised Patty didn't lobby for a beagle. She surprised me by expressing an interest in a miniature dachshund provided it had long hair. I continued my research, not wanting to consider just one option.

At one point, we seriously considered getting a Portuguese water dog. They were easy to train and care for and ranked low on the scale of dogs who shed. The problem was there weren't breeders anywhere in New York State. Michigan and New Jersey were options, however. When we learned how much it would cost to purchase a puppy and have it flown to us, we decided to abandon the idea.

I grew impatient because winter was approaching. I didn't want to have to wait until spring if it could be avoided. It was time to stop searching for an obscure breed that would impress other people. I returned to the top ten dog breed list, and there sat miniature dachshunds at number seven. Patty nodded her head when I told her we were going in that direction. By now she was amused at how much energy I was expending with this whole "we have to get a dog" thing.

Armed with conviction, I returned to the internet and found several dachshund breeders in our area. One of them had puppies that would be available in a little over two weeks. My effort shifted into overdrive. The pictures of the litter on the breeder's website were adorable. I immediately began to worry that they all might be spoken for if I dragged my feet. There were only three left to choose from. Because Patty and I worked different shifts, we would have to wait until the weekend before we could go see them. I couldn't wait that long. I had her pick out one of the three remaining puppies to ease her disappointment of not being able to go with me. I thought she made a good choice.

Lorrie was the first dog breeder I'd ever met. She was a pleasant woman who had a well-kept house. She said, "A breeder's home is also their place of business." It made sense. I guessed that she was fifteen years younger than I was, but she possessed a wealth of knowledge about dachshunds. Since this was my first experience with buying an American Kennel Club (AKC) registered puppy, I listened to her intently.

She explained that the puppies were taken to the vet at regular intervals and vaccinated and wormed according to the AKC recommendations. She also had her dogs microchipped and insisted on being kept as one of the contacts should the dog go missing. "I don't want a lost dog of mine to ever have to spend a night in an animal shelter," she said. I was impressed with her commitment to her animals.

I was caught off guard when she started asking me questions. The owner of every dog I purchased up until this point was just happy to find a home for it. I quickly sensed that if Lorrie had doubts about me being a responsible pet owner, she wasn't going to sell me one of her puppies.

She asked, "Why do you want a puppy?" "What kind of environment will you be raising it in?" "Are there any other pets in the house?" These were all intrusive questions, and I bristled at the thought of having to be interviewed just to get a puppy. But I liked the lady and forced myself to acknowledge where she was coming from.

I spotted the puppy Patty had picked out and asked if I could hold it. "It" was a "he" resting in his bed while his littermates roughhoused. My heart warmed when Lorrie placed him in my hands. The quiet little boy welcomed my attention by licking the hands that held him. My heart melted when Lorrie showered him with praises. When I handed him back to her, she called my attention to his coat. "He's a red sable," she said. I asked about the long black strands of hair beginning to grow over it. "Eventually this red coat will be completely hidden by those long black strands."

I left Lorrie with a deposit and drove home, noting the sense of elation I felt. Everything in my life was about to change. Suddenly, hope filled the void I felt after losing Lucky. My mind raced with possibilities. For the next two weeks the little red dog was all I could think about.

After the allotted time passed, I took Patty to visit Lorrie. I should have taken Patty with me the first time because the girls hit it off so well. We left with the little fellow after Lorrie took our picture while we held him. Because dachshunds were a German breed, we decided to name him Jacob Wilhelm.

"Jake" was a pint-size package. I couldn't remember the last time I held something so alive yet so small. It quickly became evident we should have prepared better for Jake's arrival. The left-over Lucky paraphernalia we had scattered around the house was too big, and all of it would need to be altered or discarded.

Lucky's old pen was big enough for a litter of puppies. Jake needed something a lot smaller. I found a cardboard box, cut a hole in the side, and placed it inside the enclosure, which took up only about a third of the space. Patty placed a blanket and a toy rubbed with the scent of his littermates inside the box. We spread newspaper over the remaining space so we could continue with his potty training.

Jake's posh accommodations lacked one important thing—a companion. It took a couple of sleep-deprived nights for us to realize it wasn't going to work having Jake sleep alone in the kitchen. I tried to remember how we got through this phase with our other dogs. Then it occurred to me we hadn't exactly gone through this before. Sheba slept in the unfinished cellar of our first house while it was being built, and Lady slept in the garage of our second house. They were allowed to sleep in our bedroom (unpenned) once they were housebroken. Lucky was the exception. He was much older and was already housebroken when he came to stay with us. After the first night he slept with Lady and Mike, Lucky weaseled his way into our bedroom.

Until Jake was housebroken, he had to stay in his pen for the night. We decided to move the pen into our bedroom, and that put an end to our woes.

It brought me great joy to watch our little "hot dog" teetering on wobbly legs, following me around the house. My love for Jake grew stronger with each passing day. I thought about him while I was at work and couldn't wait to spend time with him when I got home. Like an infant, we took turns "babysitting" him when the other person worked. When it was my turn, I maintained my routine of repairing and upgrading things around the house. That meant Jake had to brave my hammering and sawing if he wanted to be with me.

Because of his petite size and fearless nature, I referred to him as our "brave little toaster." The nickname came from the title of an animated movie I watched with our children when they were young. Our "brave little toaster" lived in a land filled with giants. He always had to look up to observe things. Yet he still managed to live a life full of joy because of his devotion to Patty and me. He trusted us to keep him safe.

We made great progress housebreaking Jake his first month with us, partly because we were vigilant and partly because the December snows were insignificant. When the snow did arrive, escorting Jake outside to do his business took on a whole new meaning. He wasn't afraid of the snow; it was just that his short little legs couldn't handle more than four inches of it. After one heavy snowfall, I found myself out shoveling off a small portion of the front lawn so he could move around enough to potty.

The rest of the winter I played with Jake indoors. The snow was just too deep for him to move around in. If I did take him out, I first had to shovel a trail through the snow for him to travel on. Patty fashioned a coat for him out of a sleeve cut off one of my old sweaters.

Just as Lorrie predicted, Jake's natural coat grew out. His red undercoat was completely hidden by long black fur. Only his feet and ears retained their reddish-brown color. Beautiful and cuddly, Jake developed a loving demeanor. His tail wagged continuously if Patty or I was present.

As he neared six months, Patty insisted that we raise Jake with table manners, meaning I couldn't offer him food while sitting at the table. I think Patty worked harder at training me than Jake. While she was busy teaching Jake good manners, I decided to teach Jake a few tricks.

When I was a child, my father taught our dachshund, Boots, to perform some tricks. Boots could roll over on command and play dead when Dad pretended to shoot him. Dad would form his hand into the shape of a pistol and yell, "Bang!" Boots responded by immediately flopping over on his side.

My first attempt at training Jake to play dead was a disaster. When I pointed a finger at him and yelled, "Bang," Jake was so overcome with my perceived hostility toward him that he ran away.

"Bill, you're scaring him." Patty said, laughing. "Look, the poor thing peed on the floor."

"That's the way my father used to do it," I replied.

"You're going to have to rethink your strategy, or he's never going to come anywhere near you ever again."

From then on, I injected enthusiasm into my voice and trained him with a happy, flowery-sounding "Bang-bang." Because Patty and I knew the backstory, we always got a good laugh out of it when Jake tried to play dead. I also had to modify Jake's "roll over" routine. Boots would lie down on his side and roll over to his other side. Each time I tried to show Jake how to do it, he spun around in a tight circle without lying down. So, the command became "round and round," which he performed regularly when he wanted a treat from us.

I noticed that holding Jake in my arms or having him sit on my lap amounted to a much more intimate experience than I had with my other dogs. When we played together, I was lying on the floor so I could be at eye level with him. Like most dogs, Jake would chase a tennis ball, but his favorite toys were stuffed animals that squeaked. The noise must have really annoyed him because when we weren't looking, he'd somehow find a way to remove the squeaker. Once he silenced the toy, he methodically chewed off all its appendages and scattered loose stuffing all over the floor.

There was one stuffed toy Jake was especially fond of, a hairy hedgehog named Buddha. Patty and I always got funny looks from our Christian friends when we referred to Jake's Buddha. We had to explain to them it had nothing to do with religion. It was just a name that came printed on the felt bow tie it wore. "Buddha" became part of Jake's vocabulary, so we kept using it. Buddha didn't squeak like the other toys he had; it honked like a goose. Maybe that's why he bonded so tightly to it. It was comical to see him use Buddha as a pillow under his chin while he napped. Buddha, devoid of appendages, was never far away. He carried it around with him much of the time.

Because we were "empty nesters," we treated Jake as if he was our third child. Consequently, our world revolved around him. As "parents" we were delighted to have Jake greet us when we came home. Jake was the only dog we owned that greeted us with a gift in his mouth, which was usually the closest stuffed animal he could find. If one wasn't handy, he'd go looking for one before officially greeting us.

I found this practice adorable and thought it was a plea to play fetch with him. So I'd pull the toy out of his mouth and toss it. Patty thought Jake might be showing me how much he appreciated my companionship by offering me a gift. "Maybe you shouldn't be tossing it away," she said. "You might be hurting his feelings." If she was right, I didn't want to risk sending him the wrong message, so I quit yanking the stuffed animals out of his mouth.

Because of Jake's small size and lovable demeanor we began to take him with us when we went out whenever possible. We were surprised by the growing number of establishments that had become "pet friendly." "Going for a ride" quickly became part of his vocabulary and ranked among his favorite phrases. I'd place him in the front seat and watch him immediately scurry over to the passenger side. He put his front paws on the armrest to prop himself up high enough to see out the window. His tail wagged like a propeller while he waited for me to start the vehicle. Then, whether by accident or on purpose, he managed to step on the power button and lower the window. Like every other dog I owned, he drank in the sights and smells of the outside world with one exception. That exception was in the car, Jake got to see the world as I did—at eye level.

~

Devotion

Labrador Retrievers were once my personal choice of dogs. I considered them *the* ultimate source of devotion. That is, until I came to understand the courage Jake's devotion required of him daily. What made him so fearless? I believe he drew courage from his devotion to Patty and me.

Jake challenged me to look at the world through his eyes, to consider how big and ominous things might look to him. I found it amazing that he could discount the size of the obstacles he faced, focusing instead on his faith in those he cared about. The courage he found in faith was a new and different way of looking at things for me (Hebrews 11:7).

It took a miniature dachshund to help me understand the courage needed for true devotion. What is devotion? By its very definition, devotion comes from spending time with the object of one's desire. Misplaced devotion eventually fails the person who counts on it, often at the worst possible time (Matthew 6:19–24). Objects are vulnerable to deterioration, malfunction, and theft. People can disappoint, fail, and betray those who put their trust in them.

One person who will never forsake or fail us is Jesus. His love and faithfulness to us are unequaled (Psalm 26:2–3). Followers who devote their time to reading about Him in the Bible, praying to Him, and worshipping Him don't view it as an obligation but as a privilege. Their devotion strengthens their faith, and faith gives wings to courage (Isaiah 40:31).

Maintaining a healthy and vibrant relationship with Jesus is paramount. For it is in the arena of relationships that the battle for devotion occurs; evil and selfishness will make every attempt to smother the love and light devoted followers of Jesus carry inside them. Money, status, addictions, and desires all vie for the heart and therefore our devotion.

Since we can't physically see Jesus (for the time being), we must rely on faith fueled by prayer and the promptings of the Holy Spirit to guide us. The Spirit speaks on behalf of Jesus (John 14:26) until the day comes when we will meet him face-to-face (Job 19:25–27). Those who follow Jesus can never be separated from this love by anything in all of creation (Romans 8:35–39).

Jake had a practice of climbing up on my stomach as I sat on the sofa watching the television. It was no accident that he placed himself directly in my line of sight. He wanted my attention. If I asked him, "What do you want?" he would just continue to stare. Invariably, I'd get up from the couch and run through a list of queries, trying to figure out what he wanted. Many times, it was an exercise in futility because the remedy remained a mystery. Was he trying to measure my level of interest when he engaged me face-to-face? Did I appreciate his devotion, or was I too distracted to notice or even care?

What is our reaction to Jesus when he tries to get our attention? Are we too distracted to notice or care? Do we have the courage to ask, "What is it you want of me, Lord?"

As of late, I have become mindful of telling Jesus how much I love him, how grateful I am for my relationship with him. Devotion is the yardstick by which my faith is measured. Because of a dog's example, I have come to understand what devotion requires of me.

Once we, too, were foolish and disobedient. We were misled and became slaves to many lusts and pleasures. Our lives were full of evil and envy, and we hated each other. But—"When God our Savior revealed his kindness and love, he saved us, not because of the righteous things we had done, but because of his mercy. (Titus 3:3–5 NLT)

But God demonstrates his own love for us in this: While we were still sinners, Christ died for us. (Romans 5:8)

He washed away our sins, giving us a new birth and a new life through the Holy Spirit." (Titus 3:5 NLT)

Therefore, if anyone is in Christ, the new creation has come: The old has gone, the new is here! (2 Corinthians 5:17)

Do not conform to the pattern of this world, but be transformed by the renewing of your mind. Then you will be able to test and approve what God's will is—his good, pleasing and perfect will (Romans 12:2)

Show me your ways, LORD, teach me your paths. Guide me in your truth and teach me, for you are God my Savior, and my hope is in you all the day long (Psalm 25:4–5).

Afterword

What is it about our dogs that endears us to them? Why do we shower them with gifts and treat them as if they were our children? Perhaps we are undone by their unquestionable love and devotion. Or maybe it's because of the contagious joy they exude or the hope and wonder we see in their eyes when they gaze at us. A dog's faith in us rests in the probability that we will love them as much as they love us.

In the short time I had Sheba, I observed her adoration for me, a genuine love that wasn't selfish. I watched her life begin as an energetic, problematic, and undisciplined puppy. It wasn't until she committed herself to me that our relationship could blossom. When the time came for us to part, the pain of being separated from her lingered for years. Sheba taught me that I could be a better husband if I learned to put Patty first.

Lady came to be with us at a time when climbing the corporate ladder defined my existence. It was also a time when Patty was juggling many responsibilities: being a wife, a mother to her children, and a working professional. In many ways Lady served as a nanny to Dan and Mike. She taught our children how to love.

Because of Lady's lifetime example I was able to see a clearer picture of what fatherhood was about.

It was under selfish pretenses that I brought Lucky home to live with us. I had no idea of the trouble he would bring into our home, nor did I anticipate that his struggle with separation anxiety would be ongoing. It took years for me to see that his struggles were not unlike my own. To learn that perfect love casts out fear. In many ways, he was the antithesis of the perfect dog, but I loved him just the same. Lucky reminded me almost daily that, like him, I was a flawed living thing in need of grace.

Dogs have been in my life now for more than a half a century. They have shown me what a better version of myself could look like. By casting aside prejudice, hate, fear, selfishness, and ingratitude, I could love others like they do. I can be a better person.

The faith, hope, joy, and love we see in the life of a dog are also tenets of the Christian faith (1 Corinthians 13:4–7). Love is the root of a relationship with "man's best friend" just as it is with a personal relationship with Jesus Christ. The Bible declares that love comes from God (1 John 4:7) because God is love (1 John 4:16). What happens when we hold the word *dog* written on a piece of paper up to a mirror? It's a reminder that a dog's love mirrors God's love.

For dogs, love is a verb, something they put into action to acknowledge the love we have shown them. What has your dog taught you about love? What action have you taken in response to that love? Have you considered the possibility that the relationship you have with your dog was designed to serve as a model for the relationship God desires to have with you?

As I mentioned earlier, the dogs I have known have made me a better person. They remind me daily that like them, I can be a bearer of the kind of love that moves my hands and feet. What kind of a place would the world be without a dog's love?

Acknowledgments

I would like to thank Jesus Christ, my Lord and Savior, for gifting me with the ability to capture words on a page and the insight to form sentences that could be used for His glory.

My thanks go out to the following people:

My loving wife and college sweetheart, Patty, for her unending love and support.

My sons, Dan and Mike, who make me proud to be their father.

My writing coach, Yvonne Kanu at WordPolish Editorial Services, for seeing the potential in my manuscript.

My editor, Deb Hall at The Write Insight, for making my manuscript sparkle.

The team at Illumify Media Global, for doing an amazing and professional job publishing and marketing my book.

My alma mater, Roberts Wesleyan University for equipping me with head knowledge and heart knowledge.

The pastors, staff, and special people at Pearce Memorial Church for their kindness and support.

About the Author

Bill lives in Western New York with his wife, Patty, and their two dachshunds, Brody and Herbie. He holds a bachelor of arts degree in biology and a master of science degree in leadership, both from Roberts Wesleyan University in Rochester, New York. After thirty-two years in the manufacturing sector, he decided to change careers to gain a better understanding of servanthood. He currently works as the assistant director of facilities at the church he also attends. He also leads a small group gathering of Christians and teaches an adult Sunday school class on occasion.

Bill has been a Christian for most of his life, having been raised in the Free Methodist Church. As a junior in high school, he rededicated his life to Jesus Christ and affirmed his faith in baptism many years later as an adult. He spends his

free time renovating a cottage, reading, researching his
family history, and fiddling with a model railroad. With
retirement just around the corner, Bill looks forward to
devoting more time to his college sweetheart Patty, genealogy
research, and writing.

Bill is also the author of *Junior's Hope: A memoir of a
Father's Son*, written as a tribute to his deceased father.
While journaling his father's last few months on earth, he
discovered his love for writing.

He maintains a blog, *Scraps*, at www.billroushey.com. Blog
posts also appear on Twitter and Instagram @billroushey.

Printed in the USA
CPSIA information can be obtained
at www.ICGtesting.com
CBHW020601210424
7249CB00004B/149